birdhouses

birdhouses

From Castles to Cottages—20 Simple Homes and Feeders to Make in a Weekend

Alison Jenkins

Reader's Digest

The Reader's Digest Association, Inc.
Pleasantville, New York/Montreal

This edition published by
The Reader's Digest Association, Inc.
by arrangement with
THE IVY PRESS LIMITED
The Old Candlemakers
Lewes, East Sussex BN7 2NZ, U.K.

FOR IVY PRESS
Creative Director: PETER BRIDGEWATER
Publisher: JASON HOOK
Art Director: KARL SHANAHAN
Senior Project Editor: CAROLINE EARLE
Design: JANE LANAWAY
Illustrations: IVAN HISSEY
Photography: CALVEY TAYLOR-HAW

FOR READER'S DIGEST
U.S. Project Editor: KIM CASEY
Canadian Project Editor: PAMELA JOHNSON
Senior Project Designer: GEORGE MCKEON
Executive Editor, Trade Publishing: DOLORES YORK
President & Publisher, Trade Publishing: HAROLD CLARKE

Address any comments about *BIRDHOUSES* to:
The Reader's Digest Association, Inc.
Adult Trade Publishing
Reader's Digest Road
Pleasantville, NY 10570-7000

For more Reader's Digest products and information,
visit our website:
www.rd.com (in the United States)
www.readersdigest.ca (in Canada)

Printed in China

1 3 5 7 9 10 8 6 4 2

NOTE TO OUR READERS
All do-it-yourself activities involve a degree of risk.
Skills, materials, tools, and site conditions vary widely.
Although the editors have made every effort to
ensure accuracy, the reader remains responsible
for the selection and use of tools, materials, and
methods. Always follow manufacturer's operating
instructions, and observe safety precautions.

Library of Congress Cataloging-in-Publication Data

Jenkins, Alison.
    Birdhouses : from castles to cottages — 20 simple homes and feeders to make in a weekend
  / Alison Jenkins.
       p. cm.
    ISBN 0-7621-0644-1
    1. Birdhouses—Design and construction. 2. Bird feeders—Design and construction. I.
  Title.

  QL676.5J43 2005
  690'.892—dc22

                                    2005052932

Contents

Introduction

This book offers you 20 unique, specially designed birdhouses and feeders inspired by different architectural styles from all over the world. From a simple log cabin to a fantastic fairy castle, all of these houses make practical homes for birds. And while they indulge human flights of fancy, each will provide roomy, comfortable accommodations for two small birds and their progeny throughout the breeding season and for years to come.

You might opt for a folly with the shape (and texture) of a sandcastle or a birdhouse in the guise of a beach cabana. Or perhaps the bird feeder inspired by a Neoclassical temple may appeal to your aesthetic sense. We've even replicated a Mississippi River

paddle steamer for any small birds with a zest for travel. Before you begin to feel nervous: You do *not* need the skills of a master carpenter to make these birdhouses. You can start with just a reasonably equipped toolbox and some common sense. We've included a "basics" section at the front of the book, and all the techniques used are explained in illustrated steps as you go. In addition, easy templates and guidelines are supplied for every project, and projects of varying difficulty are offered so you can start with the simplest and work up to something slightly more elaborate when you are ready.

Many wild birds have suffered from changes that humans have made to the environment, so it makes sense that we should try to give something back—in the form of safe places in our backyards—that will encourage wild birds to nest and breed.

How to use this book

The book falls into two parts. The first contains a guide to tools and equipment and provides step-by-step instructions for the techniques you will use, plus guidance on how to make four basic birdhouse shapes. The second part contains step-by-step instructions for 20 birdhouse and feeder projects, using not only the basic shape templates but customized and special templates, too.

Tools, equipment, techniques, and Basic Shapes

The practical section of this book begins with a guide to the tools and techniques you will need to make a birdhouse or feeder. The four basic birdhouse shapes that follow (see pages 20–27) can be assembled according to the instructions provided and then painted in one or more colors of your choice to create safe-and-sound dwellings for the wild birds in your garden. Any of the four would be a good first project for the novice birdhouse builder and require no extra templates or additions.

The projects

The first seven projects are each based on one of the four basic birdhouse shapes that is customized with small structural additions or alterations. The remaining projects use special templates and recycled objects to create equally attractive and solid end results. To offer the more adventurous or experienced craftsperson a greater challenge, the last three projects are a little more complex and unusual in shape and construction.

The templates

You will find the templates for the 20 projects on pages 156–173. All have been reduced from full size—the percentage of reduction is given under the title for each project. In order to be able to trace the full-size template, you will need to photocopy the page required, then enlarge it by the given percentage on a copying machine. Next trace the template and cut it out carefully. Retain the original copy as a reference.

BIRDHOUSES USING THE BASIC SHAPES

Beach Cabana

Gingerbread Cottage

Log Cabin

Church

Cinderella's Castle

Haunted House

Swiss Chalet

Each of these designs uses Basic Shape 1, 2, 3, or 4 as a starting point. The basic templates have been customized, extended, or embellished with extra structural or decorative details.

BIRDHOUSES AND FEEDERS USING SPECIAL TEMPLATES

Neoclassical Temple

Sandcastle

Pyramid

Space Rocket

Tea Party Feeder

Swimming Pool Feeder

Tower Feeder

Mediterranean Feeder,

High-Rise Feeder

Modernist Villa

Diner

Bandstand Feeder

These birdhouses and feeders don't use the basic shapes at all, but instead have special templates of their own. In addition to the construction materials you'd expect— lumber and plywood, for example—we've also creatively incorporated recycled materials such as plastic and toy balls.

Tools and Equipment

Because this book is aimed at the novice woodworker, it is understood that you probably will not have a fully equipped workshop at your disposal. Any of the birdhouses and feeders described in the following chapters can be made using the equipment and materials listed here—all are inexpensive and readily available from a home-repair or hardware store. Most households will have the basics, such as a hammer, screwdrivers, a drill, and more, and there are a few specialty additions, such as a miter saw—an invaluable and inexpensive tool to buy. Browse through the list to make sure you have everything you need, then try out the basic techniques step by step, using some spare pieces of plywood, to familiarize yourself with the methods required. Remember: Practice makes perfect.

Basic tool kit

AWL: An invaluable hand tool, used for making holes in lumber or other materials, for making pilot holes before inserting a screw, and for marking drill-hole positions.

CHISEL: A small chisel allows easy shaping of awkward areas where access with a jigsaw blade would be difficult. Simply use the blade to cleanly chop away excess wood.

ELECTRIC DRILL: A power drill is an essential piece of equipment when making holes of all different sizes. Some drills come with screwdriver bits for inserting and removing screws. Choose a set of multipurpose twist bits to match your drill, plus a few spade bits for making larger holes (for birdhouse entrances or as sockets

for dowel supports or perches). Add a countersink bit to complete the collection (for making recesses so the screw heads lie flush with your surface material for a neat and professional finish).

HACKSAW: A small, handheld saw, useful for cutting plastics, narrow dowels, or strips of wood.

HAMMER: A medium-weight hammer is useful for knocking in nails and paneling nails. Do not use one that feels too heavy in your hand— you're likely to bend the nails and spoil the appearance of your birdhouse.

JIGSAW: A power jigsaw makes light work of cutting straight and curved shapes from sheet materials such as plywood, which is used in the construction of most of the birdhouses. Choose a multipurpose blade set to match your jigsaw, including blades for both fine, curved work and fast, straight cutting.

MARKER PEN: A waterproof permanent marker may be used to make thick lines as decorative detail on birdhouse exteriors and for marking drill-hole positions on plastic.

PAINTBRUSHES: Ordinary household paintbrushes can be used to apply primer and basecoats, while finer artist's paintbrushes are best to add any decorative details.
Tip: Use a cotton swab for adding small spots of paint.

PALETTE: A small plate or saucer is handy to keep by your side when painting in decorative details. You can use it to transfer small amounts of paint from larger cans.

PENCIL AND RULER: No toolbox should be without equipment for accurate marking and measuring. A metal straightedge or ruler with both imperial and metric markings is the most useful. Remember to keep your pencils sharp!

PUTTY KNIFE: A flexible wide-blade knife used for applying wood filler to joints and uneven surfaces.

SCREWDRIVERS: A comprehensive set, containing both slotted and Phillips (cross-head) screwdrivers in a variety of different sizes, is handy. This will ensure that you can drive in and remove just about any screw.

SCISSORS: A medium-sized pair of paper scissors will be needed for cutting the paper templates.

STAPLER: A handy tool to have at your disposal for attaching lightweight materials firmly in place.

UTILITY KNIFE: A knife with a retracting blade is used for general cutting and scoring. Keep the blade retracted when not in use.

Specialty tools

MITER SAW: An extremely useful piece of equipment for making accurate angled and straight cuts in lumber. The saw is fixed to a miter box—simply adjust the handle to move the blade to the required angle.

TIN SNIPS: A tool with strong, sharp blades suitable for cutting thin sheet metal.

Materials

EXTERIOR-GRADE PLYWOOD: Always use good-quality marine plywood for birdhouse constructions. Most of the projects use ½ inch (12-mm)-thick plywood, unless otherwise stated. A few pieces need to be cut from other sizes, but this is clearly stated on the cutting guide and templates provided.

We have used standard 2 x 4-ft (61 x 122-cm)-long sheets throughout—where instructions state half a sheet or smaller, it is simply this size sheet cut in half or smaller.
Tip: Take your cutout templates to the lumberyard and buy only enough plywood for your needs, or purchase a few small pieces cheaply.

PAINT: Any latex-based exterior-quality paint or artist's acrylic paint is suitable for decorating your birdhouses—a good opportunity to use up all the leftovers after home-decorating projects. Avoid oil-based paints or those with strong odors because this may deter some birds. It is not necessary to paint the interiors: The birds aren't that fussy!

PLAIN PAPER FOR TEMPLATES: Any thin paper will suffice. Choose large sheets so that you don't need to make joints. Newspaper can also be used, if you don't have easy access to plain paper.

PRIMER/UNDERCOAT: All the bare plywood pieces used in the construction of the birdhouse projects must be suitably primed. This seals and prepares the wooden surface before the application of the decorative topcoats. For best results, use two or three coats of primer. Between each coat, sand the surface smooth and wipe away the dust with a soft cloth.

SANDPAPER: Use coarse or medium-grade sandpaper for taking off rough edges and splinters from cut pieces, then use a finer-grade sheet for finishing.

WATERPROOF WOOD GLUE: The glue used in the construction of all the projects must be waterproof because the birdhouses are intended for exterior use. Apply the glue liberally, wiping away any excess with a damp cloth when the joint is secure. Always allow the glue to dry completely before applying primer or paint.

WOOD FILLER: Use an exterior-quality product to fill joints and to smooth out any surface imperfections. Also, when you cut plywood, you may see holes or gaps between the layers. These are known as "voids" and should be filled, or they may allow moisture to penetrate into the wood, which will cause damage.

NAILS, SCREWS, AND HARDWARE

Screw sizes are given as a number followed by the length measurement. The number denotes the diameter of the screw. The smaller the number, the smaller the diameter of the screw shaft. Measurements for nails and hinges denote the length only.

For the birdhouse doors you will also require a turn button—a small rectangular metal bar that has a screw hole in the center. The button is screwed to the fixed frame of the birdhouse opposite the hinged side of the door or flap, it is then rotated on the screw to hold the door/flap in a closed position.

Basic Techniques

The essence of this book is simplicity, and all of the projects are aimed at the beginner rather than a highly skilled craftsperson. All you need to do is master a few basic skills and techniques that are shown in step-by-step form over the next few pages, and you'll be able to make any birdhouse that captures your imagination! A word of advice—don't be too hard on yourself if your first attempts are disappointing. It takes time to learn and become proficient at any new skill.

> **TIP**
>
> *Always double-check measurements and markings before cutting—you can alter pencil marks, but you can't undo a cut!*

Accuracy and safety

While accuracy of cutting and joining is necessary to achieve a good result, do not be disheartened if your first attempts are not as good as they could be—practice makes perfect! Take care in tracing and cutting out the templates, then transfer all of the design and cutting details to your plywood sheet just as carefully. Small inaccuracies in the template stage will be amplified when it comes to the cutting stage.

Safety is paramount when using all tools. Use your hand and power tools with care and respect. Never change drill bits or blades when your power tool is turned on, and always use blade guards on cutting tools. It is advisable to use a dust mask when working with lumber or sheet materials to avoid inhaling small particles. To protect your eyes from flying splinters, safety goggles are also essential when working with the hacksaw and jigsaw. Work outside or in a well-ventilated space.

A sturdy workbench is a great asset, and it can make cutting and drilling much easier. Look for one that can be adjusted for height in order to prevent back strain. It also prevents any damage to interior surfaces, such as kitchen countertops or tables.

Using a drill

A power drill is a must in anyone's toolbox, not just for birdhouse construction but also for general home repair and maintenance.

Making a pilot hole using an awl

After clearly marking the hole position with a pencil dot, place the point of the awl on the hole position; then press firmly into the surface using a twisting action. This ensures that the drill bit will not slip. The same method can be used to insert small screws that do not require predrilled holes.

Drilling a pilot hole

Place the point of the bit into the marker hole. Ensure that the drill is straight and upright; then begin drilling using a light downward pressure. Use a slow speed at first; then increase it to complete the hole. This small hole can be used as a pilot for a screw to join one section to another, or for securing dowel supports or hinges.

Drilling a countersink hole

A "countersink" bit is used to create a shallow recess that allows the head of a screw to sit flush with the surrounding surface. The surface can be filled and sanded smooth to completely conceal the screw. Place the tip of the bit into the pilot hole, then drill for a second or two to make the shallow recess required.

Making larger diameter holes

A spade bit creates large access holes for the birdhouses, and for a jigsaw blade. Place the tip of the bit into a predrilled pilot hole. Drill slowly at first; then increase the speed to complete the hole. To prevent the underside of the wood from splintering, place the section to be drilled on a spare piece of plywood.

Inserting a screw

Place the tip of the screw in the predrilled hole; then hold the screw with one hand and turn it a few times using a screwdriver with the other. When the screw seems firm, brace the section to be joined with one hand and drive the screw in.

Finishing

After driving in the screw, run your finger over the surface to make sure that the head does not protrude. If it does, screw it down a little more. You can now fill the hole with wood filler, then sand smooth when dry.

Using a jigsaw

A power jigsaw is invaluable for cutting and shaping sheet materials. By using suitable blades, you can make straight and curved cuts according to the template shape.

Straight cuts and windows

This jigsaw is fitted with a blade suitable for fast, straight cutting. To cut out a piece inside a section, you must first use a spade bit to drill a hole at each corner that is large enough to allow the blade to pass through. Insert the blade into the first hole and cut carefully along the bead toward the next hole. Do this on all four sides until the maneuver is complete.

Curved cuts

The blade used for curved cuts is narrower and finer than the one used for ordinary straight cutting. To follow a curve on a template outline, place the moving blade on the outline and proceed carefully. To achieve a good result, move the jigsaw along slowly while using a fast cutting speed. To cut out a circular window, drill a large pilot hole inside and next to the outline, then insert the blade. Follow the curved bead carefully to cut out the circular shape.

Angled cuts

Jigsaws have an adjustable baseplate. The baseplate can be swiveled to one side or the other to enable angled cuts. The degree of the angle can be varied as the pattern requires.

HELPFUL HINT

Make sure that the motor is running before the jigsaw makes contact with the material to be cut.

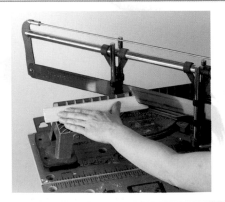

Using a miter saw

A miter saw is used for making both accurate straight cuts and angled cuts of varying degrees. Simply mark the section of lumber to be cut then place it onto the saw under the cutting blade.

Adjust the angle of the blade using the lever situated under the saw.

Joints

Most of the birdhouses are constructed very simply—the cut pieces are first glued together, then made more secure with paneling nails or screws.

Gluing the joint

Squeeze a generous bead of wood glue to one half of the joint. Press the second piece firmly to the bead, allowing the excess glue to seep out of the joint—this can be wiped away with a damp cloth later. While the glue is still wet, you may make adjustments to ensure that the pieces are aligned correctly.

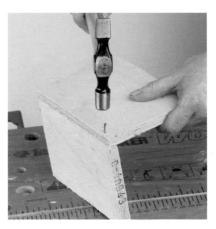

Securing the joint

When the glue has set a little and is holding the joint together, you can insert paneling nails at intervals of approximately 2 inches (5 cm) along the length of the joint. It is good practice to insert a nail at each end of the joint first, then a few at intervals in between.

To use screws to make a joint, you must first drill pilot holes and then insert the fixing screws. This is more time-consuming but it is very effective.

Filling and sanding

It is essential that all gaps are properly filled and all surfaces are smooth before primer or paint is applied.

1

Apply the wood filler to the joint or surface using a flexible putty knife. Press the filler down into any crack. Scrape away any excess filler using the blade of the knife; then allow it to dry completely.

2

Rub a sheet of medium or coarse sandpaper over the surface to take off lumps. Use a fine-grade sandpaper to smooth the surface further and create a sound base for the primer and paint.

PRIMING

The application of a primer is necessary to seal and prepare the bare wooden surface. Apply a thin, even coat using a household paintbrush. Sand the surface smooth using a fine-grade paper when it is dry. Wipe away dust particles using a damp cloth and then apply a second coat. Repeat if a third coat is required.

Bring in the Birds

Feeding and creating homes for wild birds is a hobby enjoyed by many people. You may wish to start on a small scale with a simple fruit garland hung from a tree branch or make a tiny birdhouse to fill a sheltered space in your backyard. Or you may try to build a larger birdhouse in the hope of reaping greater bird-watching rewards! Whichever route you take, these tips will help you to achieve success.

Feeding

It is a popular misconception that the more food you put out, the more birds you'll attract to your garden. In fact, birds are choosy about what they eat—even if they're hungry. Many people rely on premixed feed, but a little thought toward menu creation will attract a wider variety of birds. Birds require water in addition to food, so always provide a container of fresh water either inside or close to your feeder.

Try to include several feeders in your garden—it sometimes pays to diversify. You can never be entirely sure with birds because they can be fickle—some will readily visit a low-level feeding table, while others are happy just to peck at fruit dangling from a tree branch. Some, on the other hand, will devour anything they can get their beaks on. Make sure that you provide a variety of foods and a means of delivery to cater for all visitors. Bird-feed tips and recipes are featured on the feeder project pages.

SEASONAL FEEDING

All birds need to generate a large amount of energy all year round and that means constantly finding and consuming a large quantity of food. During the summer and fall months there will usually be a plentiful supply of natural food in the form of seeds and fruit. Do not, however, assume that this will be sufficient and stop leaving food out completely during this time of plenty. Just modify your feeding slightly according to the season. Use the chart below as a guideline to seasonal feeding:

Winter
It is very important to include lots of high-energy fats like peanut butter and suet, as well as seed mixes and bread in your feeder at this time of year, when natural food is scarce.

Spring
This season also requires lots of high-energy fat mixes as well as seeds and scraps. If you attract lots of birds during the spring, they will usually stay throughout the year.

Summer
In warmer weather conditions, always be sure that there is a regular supply of fresh water in your garden. While natural food is plentiful, you should stock your feeder with light seed mixes, scraps, fruit, and bread.

Fall
This is a great time to attract some migrating birds on their way to warmer climates. Some fruit and berries will still be available in the wild, but you should basically offer your winter feeding menu with less emphasis on high-energy fat and seed mixtures.

raisins

millet

Top tips for attracting birds to your garden

Providing food and water alone is not enough to make your garden attractive to wild birds. Every effort must be taken to provide a safe, sheltered environment in which the birds can feed, roost, and nest. Carefully considered plantings and a well-planned maintenance routine will improve the chances of your garden becoming a haven for wild birds and their families throughout the year.

The region in which you live will play a part in determining which birds you are likely to see. To encourage them to pay you a visit, plant lots of native species of plants and shrubs, especially woody climbers such as roses, wisteria, honeysuckle, or other plants that are typical to your area. Too many unusual varieties may have an adverse effect and may discourage the birds even though they may look beautiful. Conifers of all varieties are particularly useful additions to your garden plan. These evergreens can be shelter and protection for nesting, roosting, and perching all year, and in addition, produce cones in the spring that will ripen beautifully in the summer to provide a plentiful food source.

Let Mother Nature provide bird food free of charge. Take advantage of plants, trees, or shrubs that bear fruit or berries—birds will flock to feed when the time is right. Keep an eye on your fruit trees, however, if you intend to harvest some for your own use—a flock of hungry birds can very quickly strip a tree of fruit, leaving none for you!

blueberries

sunflower seeds

Stock up with fruit, berries, and high-energy seed mixes to attract feathered friends to your bird feeder.

As the year draws to an end, resist the temptation to cut back your plants in readiness for the winter, especially seed-bearing varieties. Leave them untrimmed for a while and give the birds a chance to help themselves. Eager gardeners should also resist the temptation to be too tidy. Do not get rid of dry leaves and branches—simply sweep them into heaps at the corner of the garden to provide cover for insects, which in turn provide food for the birds. The dead organic material can also be a very useful source of nesting material.

Try to avoid using chemical products or insecticides in your garden as a means to control pests or weeds. They are extremely harmful to the environment in general, and are detrimental to birds and other wildlife. Search your local garden centers for organic or natural products as alternatives.

MAINTENANCE

Once a year, during the fall when the weather begins to turn colder, you should empty your birdhouse of any debris and old nesting materials. Old feces and stale seed or rotting food can be a haven for germs , disease, and parasites which can, if not removed, be passed on to the next family that may take up residence the following season. Simply remove the box from its position; then remove the screw that holds the base flap secure to gain access to the interior. If the access flap has a turn button or a hook fastener, this job is even

easier—there's no need for the screwdriver at all. Once all the debris has been removed, scrub the interior using a small, stiff brush and some soapy water and allow the box to dry completely. When it is dry, resecure the access flap, and you can use this opportunity to touch up any faded paintwork or make any necessary repairs. Remount the birdhouse in preparation for the spring when the same birds may return, or you may even see some new faces in your birdhouse.

Basic Shapes

Now that you've mastered a few basic techniques, you can begin the task of making a birdhouse. The four shapes on the following pages are the basis for a wide variety of customized birdhouses and feeders. Just add any detailing you choose.

Customizing your birdhouse

Try to look at these Basic Shapes as blank canvases. You can paint them in any color combination that strikes your fancy. Choose one of the decorative styles from the project pages or even try a more adventurous approach by adding architectural features and design details. As your confidence grows and your skills improve, you may like to design some features of your own, such as uniquely shaped chimneys or windows. Remember, the birds aren't concerned with the color of their new home—all they'll care about is that it's a dry and safe place in which to raise their young.

All of the birdhouse designs in this book can be decorated to suit your taste and scaled up to attract larger birds.

Access hole sizes

The size of the access hole will determine the type of bird that will visit the birdhouse. The houses in this book are mainly designed for small birds—see the chart to the right. However, you just never know with birds: you may be pleasantly surprised in the spring when the birds start house hunting—more unusual species may take a liking to your accommodation.

Big ideas

If you would like to entice some larger feathered friends to visit your backyard, you will need to "scale up" a little. The templates of the four basic birdhouses can be enlarged by 150 or even 200 percent in order to accommodate a bigger bird. The access hole can also be made larger.

Hole diameter	Birds
1–1½ in. (2.5–4 cm)	*bluebirds, chickadees, flycatchers, house sparrows, nuthatches, swallows, warblers, wrens*
1½–2 in. (4–5 cm)	*barn swallows, finches, martins, phoebes, sparrows*
2½–3 in. (6–7.5 cm)	*redheaded woodpeckers, common and northern flickers*
3 in. (7.5 cm)	*screech owls, woodpeckers*

NOTE: To drill large-diameter holes you will need a hole-saw attachment for your drill.

Display

How you decide to display your birdhouse depends on personal preference and, of course, your circumstances. If you live in an apartment or small home and do not have a backyard, the pole-mounted option may not be for you—perhaps a wall-hung box on your terrace or a small tabletop feeder on your patio would suit your requirements better.

Safety is important when choosing a good location for a birdhouse or feeder. You need to place it where the birds can gain access (and where you can see them), but also where other creatures, like squirrels or raccoons, cannot! These visitors are rather partial to bird eggs and young and therefore should be deterred. Squirrels in particular can be very persistent, so make the access hole as small as possible in order to keep the predators out.

Any wall-hung or pole-mounted birdhouse should be at least 6–10 feet (1.8–3 meters) above ground level to discourage small predators from visiting. You may apply grease to the post or pole to make it even more difficult for small, undesirable animals to make their way up to the birdhouse.

See the hints and suggestions with each project for alternatives and display ideas.

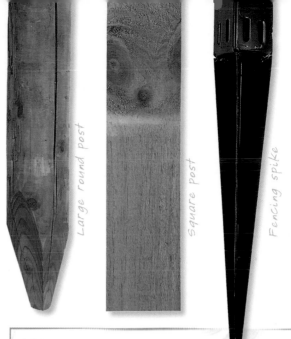

Large round post

Square post

Fencing spike

SECURING THE POLE IN THE GROUND

There are two ways to make sure that your pole stands firm in the ground. You can drive a metal fence-post spike into the ground and then engage the pole into it. Or, you can dig a hole in the ground, insert the pole, support it in a vertical position, and then fill the hole with ready-mixed mortar. Just add water to the mix and wait for it to set. While the mortar mix is beginning to set, check that the pole is truly vertical with a level and adjust the position of the post/pole, if necessary. You won't be able to do this after the mortar has set! Remove the supports when the pole is secure.

WALL HANGING

Screw sturdy brass hanging brackets to the back of the box, then screw these securely to the wall. If the wall is made of brick or stone, be sure to use suitable wall anchors.

POST/POLE MOUNTING

A 3 x 3-inch (7.5 x 7.5-cm) square or large round fence post is ideal for mounting your birdhouse. Use three or four long screws to secure a piece of plywood that is a little smaller than the base of the house or feeder to the top of the post; then screw the overhang directly into the house/feeder base.

If your garden is frequented by small predators such as squirrels, cats, or rodents, secure a predator guard to the post or pole. These clever devices are available from pet stores—some look like lamp shades that fit neatly around the pole. The aim is to prevent undesirables from climbing up the pole to gain access to the feeder or birdhouse.

A cheap, do-it-yourself alternative is to slip a length of plastic downspout over the post before attaching the birdhouse or feeder to the top. The plastic surface of the downspout is slippery and will deter all but the most persistent and ingenious small animals, particularly squirrels, from making their way up to the birdhouse.

Basic Shape 1

This small wall-hung box with a sloping, hinged access lid is a perfect first project. The pieces are small and easy to handle, and this design offers a good opportunity for some cutting practice using the jigsaw—on both straight and angled cuts—as well as general construction and drill work.

You will need:

- basic tool kit and equipment (*see pages 8–11*)
- one sheet ½-in. (12-mm)-thick plywood—2 x 4 ft (61 x 122 cm)
- spade bit 1–1½ in. (2.5 x 3.8 cm) diameter
- wood glue
- two 1-in. (2.5-cm) brass hanging brackets, plus screws
- two 1½-in. (38-mm) brass flush hinges, plus screws
- approx. thirty 1-in. (2.5-cm) paneling nails

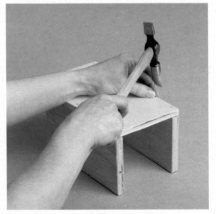

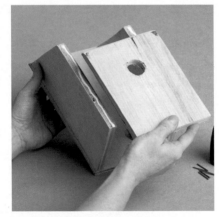

1

Place the front section faceup on a piece of waste plywood. Locate the pencil dot that indicates the drill hole and the center of the access hole. Make a small pilot hole using the sharp point of the awl on the pencil dot. Insert the point of the spade bit into the pilot hole and carefully drill the entrance hole. The waste piece of plywood will prevent the back of the material from splintering. Sand the edges of the entrance hole smooth.

2

Set the back section on your work surface with the inner face toward you, and apply a bead of wood glue close to both side edges. Place the side pieces onto the glue and press down firmly.

When the glue has set a little, turn the shape over and hammer a few paneling nails through the back section and down into the side walls, at intervals of approximately 2 inches (5 cm).

Note: Make sure that the nails are hammered in straight—if they are crooked the sharp points will break through the surface of the side wall as they penetrate.

3

Turn the shape over again and apply a bead of glue to the edges of the side walls as shown. Press the front section into position. Secure the front to the back and sides using paneling nails, at intervals of about 2 inches (5 cm). If any glue seeps out, it can be wiped away easily using a damp cloth.

First Steps | Trace and enlarge the template provided on page 156 to full size. Next cut out the pieces and transfer the outlines to a sheet of ½-inch (12-mm)-thick plywood, making sure to mark any drill-hole positions with pencil dots. Carefully cut out the pieces using a jigsaw. Use a medium-grade sandpaper to smooth any rough or splintered edges.

4

Check the fit of the base section to the box. If your cutting is slightly less than perfect you may find that the base is a little too large. This is not a problem— glue the base in position and nail securely as before; then use a sheet of rough-grade sandpaper to take off the excess so the edges lie flush with the birdhouse walls. If the base is more than a little too large (or too small), you may need to cut another section more accurately.

5

With the house on its back, set the access lid/roof section next to it as shown. Place the brass hinge by the lid and back wall— roughly in the center. Mark the drill holes with pencil dots, using the holes in the hinge flanges as a guide. Remove the hinge; then use your awl to make pilot holes at each pencil dot. You may find it easier to use a fine drill bit on an electric drill to make these small pilot holes. After replacing the hinge in position, carefully drive in each screw to hold it secure.

6

Position each hanging bracket about 1–2 inches (2.5–5 cm) down from the top edge. Mark the screw holes with pencil dots, then use your awl to make pilot holes at each dot. Replace the brackets in position, and drive in the screws to securely hold them in place.

Basic Shape 2

This classic "house" shape is rectangular with a pitched roof and a hinged access door in the base. The access hole is made close to the top of the gable end of the shape, and you can add a small perch if you choose (see Basic Shape 3 for guidelines). This simple shape is ideal for customization and paint-effect decoration.

You will need:

- basic tool kit and equipment (*see pages 8–11*)
- one sheet ½-in. (12-mm)-thick plywood—2 x 4 ft (61 x 122 cm)
- spade bit 1–1½ in. (2.5–3.8 cm) diameter
- wood glue
- two 1½-in. (38-mm) brass flush hinges, plus screws
- approx. fifty 1-in. (2.5-cm) paneling nails

1

Apply a bead of wood glue close to both side edges of the back section. Place one short edge of each side section onto the glue and press firmly into position. When the glue has set a little, turn the shape over and hammer in a few paneling nails at 2-inch (5-cm) intervals to securely hold the joint.

2

Lay the shape on its back. Apply a bead of wood glue along the short edge of each side section as shown; then place the front section into position. While the glue is still wet, you can adjust the section so the lower edges match the side walls and the joint is straight. Press firmly and allow the glue to set a little. Hammer in paneling nails. Wipe away any excess glue with a damp cloth.

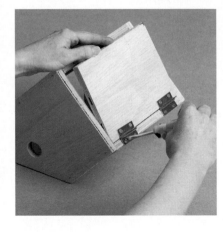

3

Check the fit of the rectangular base flap to the base. It should be snug but not too tight, and there should not be any large gaps around the edges. Sand away any irregularities around the edge of the flap with coarse-grade sandpaper and check the fit again.

Place the two hinges to the side wall and base flap, approximately 1 inch (2.5 cm) from the edge of the flap, and mark the screw-hole positions with pencil dots. Make a pilot hole at each dot using an awl, and screw the hinges into position.

First Steps | Trace and enlarge the template provided

on page 156 to full size. Next cut out the pieces and

transfer the outlines to a sheet of ½-inch (12-mm)-thick

plywood, making sure to mark any drill-hole positions

with pencil dots. Carefully cut out the pieces using a

jigsaw. Use a medium-grade sandpaper to smooth any rough or splintered edges. Drill the

access hole in position on the front using the technique described for Basic Shape 1.

> **NOTE**
>
> *This shape can be wall mounted if the roof sections are fixed so that the back edges lie flush with the back wall of the house. In this case, you may use a turn button to secure the base flap instead of a brass bracket.*

4

To keep the base flap in a closed position, you may use a brass turn button. Screw the button into the side wall approximately halfway across, then turn it clockwise to secure the flap. If you want to mount the house on a post, use the bracket method given for Basic Shape 1.

5

Now for the roof. One roof section is slightly narrower than the other to allow for an overlap at the apex so a secure weatherproof joint can be made at this point.

Select the narrowest roof section first. Apply a bead of wood glue to the diagonal edges of the front and back. Place the roof section in position as shown, making sure that the apex edge matches the point of the gable front and back. There is also a small overhang allowed front and back, so make sure that this is equal. Carefully nail the roof in place.

6

Apply a bead of wood glue along the apex edge of the narrower roof section; then carefully position the remaining wider roof section. This time the apex edge of the roof section should correspond with the edge of the narrower section to create an overlap at the apex. Secure the roof with paneling nails along the apex and front and back diagonal edges.

Basic Shape 3

This tall, narrow house is square in plan with a pitched roof and a rear access door. The design will accommodate two bird families. The access door opens to both accommodation compartments when it is time for a fall cleaning.

You will need:

- basic tool kit and equipment (*see pages 8–11*)
- one sheet 1/2-in. (12-mm)-thick plywood—2 x 4 ft (61 x 122 cm)
- spade bit 1–1 1/2 in. (2.5 x 3.8 cm) diameter
- wood glue
- 4-in. (10-cm) piece of 1/4-in. (6-mm) diameter dowel
- approx. fifty 1-in. (2.5-cm) paneling nails
- two 1-in. (2.5-cm) brass hanging brackets, plus fixing screws
- two 1 1/2-in. (38-mm) brass flush hinges, plus fixing screws
- one 1/2-in. (1.25-cm) brass hook-and-eye catch, plus fixing screws

1

Glue and nail the sides to the front section using the method described for Basic Shapes 1 and 2 (*see pages 20–23*). Check the fit of the base—it should slot in snugly between the walls and the front section. Use sandpaper to smooth away any irregularities at the edges. Apply glue to three sides of the base, then position carefully. Nail the base securely in place.

2

Take the floor partition and check that it fits snugly in place, matching the edges up with the dotted indication lines. Adjust any irregularities around the edges with coarse sandpaper, then glue the partition in place.

Hammer in a few paneling nails to hold the partition in place. This can be a little tricky, so you may like to mark the position on the outside of the house so your nails won't miss their target.

3

Lay the birdhouse on its front to place the back access flap/wall in position. Mark the screw holes for the two brass hinges with pencil dots as described for Basic Shape 2 (*see pages 22–23*). Make pilot holes using your awl at each dot; then screw the hinges securely in position. Each hinge should lie approximately 1 inch (2.5 cm) in from the edges of the section as shown above.

First Steps | Trace and enlarge the template provided on page 157 to full size. Next cut out the pieces and transfer outlines to a sheet of ½-inch (12-mm)-thick plywood. Mark any drill-hole positions with pencil dots and the partition position with dotted lines. Carefully cut out the pieces using a jigsaw. Use a medium-grade sandpaper to smooth any rough edges. Drill two access holes on the front, using the technique described for Basic Shape 1.

NOTE

This shape can also be wall-mounted. To do this simply screw a brass hanging bracket to the back of the birdhouse approximately 2 inches (5 cm) down from the eaves on each side. See Basic Shape 1 on pages 20–21 for instructions.

4

Stand the house up and mark the position of the securing catch—you may choose to use one or two catches. Pierce a pilot hole about halfway across the edge of the side wall; then screw the small eye in place. Screw the hook part of the catch to the door in a position to correspond with the eye.

5

The roof is secured by the method described for Basic Shape 2 on page 23. The narrower section is glued and nailed to the house first, then the wider one is secured. For this house, the roof must be positioned so that the edges lie flush with the back wall/access flap to allow it to open, and also to facilitate wall hanging, if required.

6

This house benefits from a perch outside each entrance hole. These are 2-inch (5-cm) lengths of dowel inserted into predrilled holes. Make a pilot hole in the correct position using the awl; then drill a hole matching the diameter of the dowel through the front wall. Apply glue to one end of each dowel, then insert it into the hole. Use a hammer to tap it in, if necessary.

To post mount the birdhouse, refer to the instructions on page 19.

Basic Shape 4
A stylish variation on a classic theme, this house has a longer and higher pitched roof and slightly sloping side walls. The slightly larger interior area is rectangular. The access flap is situated on the base of the house as in Basic Shape 2.

You will need:

- basic tool kit and equipment (*see pages 8–11*)
- one sheet ½-in. (12-mm)-thick plywood—2 x 4 ft (61 x 122 cm)

- spade bit 1–1½ in. (2.5 x 3.8 cm) diameter
- wood glue
- approx. fifty 1-in. (2.5-cm) brass hanging bracket, plus screws

- two 1½-in. (38-mm) brass flush hinges, plus fixing screws
- approx. fifty 1-in. (2.5-cm) paneling nails
- two 1-in. (2.5-cm) brass hanging brackets, plus fixing screws (optional) for wall mounting

1

Make a pilot hole using your awl, then drill the large entrance hole. Use medium-grade sandpaper to smooth any rough edges around the entrance hole.

2

Lay the front section of the birdhouse with the inner face toward you, then glue the side walls to the front section using the method described in the three previous Basic Shapes. Once the glue has set a little, turn the shape over so it stands on the side walls. Nail the joints securely at 2-inch (5-cm) intervals, then wipe away any excess glue.

3

With the birdhouse on its back, apply a bead of wood glue along the edge of the side walls. Carefully place the front section in position and firmly press in place. Hammer in paneling nails to secure the joints at intervals of 2 inches (5 cm). Check that all excess glue has been wiped away before proceeding to the next stage.

First Steps | Trace and enlarge the template provided on page 157 to full size. Next cut out the pieces and transfer outlines to a sheet of ½-inch (12-mm)-thick plywood, making sure to mark any drill-hole positions with pencil dots. Carefully cut out the pieces carefully using a jigsaw. Use a medium-grade sandpaper to smooth any rough or splintered edges.

NOTE

This shape can be wall mounted if the roof sections are adjusted so that the back edges lie flush with the back section of the house. In this case, use a turn button to secure the base flap instead of a brass bracket.

A perch can be added just below the entrance hole—see step 6, Basic Shape 3 on pages 24–25.

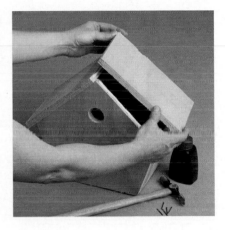

4

Turn the house over so it lies on its front. Check the fit of the base flap on the base of the house, adjusting any irregularities around the edges by using coarse-grade sandpaper. It should fit snugly but not too tightly. Mark the screw hole positions for both hinges on the flap with pencil dots. Pierce pilot holes at each dot using the awl, and screw the hinges securely into place.

5

To fix the base flap in a closed position, you may use a brass hanging bracket placed about halfway along the flap. Turn the box over and position the lower edge of the bracket (this will have two holes) to the flap, making sure that the top (this will have one hole) lies across the lower edge of the side wall.

Mark the holes as before; then screw the bracket to the base flap. Check that the flap opens and closes correctly, then screw the bracket to the side wall. To open the flap for cleaning in the fall, remove the final screw.

6

Use the method described for Basic Shapes 2 and 3 (*see pages 23 and 25*) to secure the two roof sections to the main body of the birdhouse. Use plenty of wood glue and paneling nails to hold them in place, since the pieces are larger in size than in previous shapes. The design of the roof allows a narrow overhang at the front and back, so make sure that this is equal before you insert the securing nails.

Projects

Beach Cabana

What could be more delightful than a row of cheerful, striped beach cabanas adorning the wall of your home? Three bird families can easily be accommodated inside—you could even make two or more identical boxes and hang them up side by side, creating a whole row of happy homes. This design is an extension of Basic Shape 1 (*see pages 20–21*), which is a single unit. If these pastel shades do not coordinate with the exterior color scheme of your home, choose two colors or tones that match in a more pleasing way.

You will need:

- basic tool kit (*see pages 8–11*)
- plain paper for templates
- Basic Shape 1 template (*see page 156*), Beach Cabana template (*see page 158*)
- one sheet ½-in. (12-mm)-thick plywood—2 x 4 ft (61 x 122 cm)
- wood glue
- approx. fifty 1-in. (2.5-cm) paneling nails
- wood filler
- 40-oz. (1-l) can primer
- medium- and fine-grade sandpaper
- 40-oz. (1-l) cans of yellow and pink latex-based exterior-grade paint
- ¾-in. (2-cm) masking tape
- two 1½-in. (38-mm) brass flush hinges, plus fixing screws
- two 1-in. (2.5-cm) brass hanging brackets, plus fixing screws
- household and artist's paintbrushes

First Steps | Trace and enlarge the templates provided on page 156 for Basic

Shape 1 to full size; then cut out the paper pattern pieces and transfer the outlines to

a sheet of ½-inch (12-mm)-thick plywood. Be sure to mark any drill-hole positions

with pencil dots, and the two partition positions with dotted pencil lines. Cut out

the pieces carefully using a jigsaw. Use a medium-grade sandpaper to smooth any

1

Use the method described for Basic Shape 1 (*see pages 20–21*) to assemble the front, back, sides, and base to create the birdhouse shape. Fill all joints and voids with wood filler, then sand smooth when dry. Wipe away any dust particles using a damp cloth before applying the first coat of primer to the bare wooden surfaces.

When the first coat is dry, sand it smooth using a fine-grade paper, then apply a second coat. A third coat of primer is optional. Apply primer to the lid section in the same way.

2

Because this birdhouse is designed to accommodate three bird families, two partitions are inserted to divide the units. These partitions do not need to be primed or painted. After checking the fit of each partition, apply a bead of wood glue to the lower and side edges, then slide the partition into place. Adjust the position while the glue is still wet, using your dotted pencil lines as a guide.

3

Allow the glue to set a little, so the divisions do not slide around when you move the box. Lay the box on its back, then insert two paneling nails through the front section into each division to hold it securely in place. Flip the box over and lay it on the front, repeating the process so the partition is held firmly from the front and back.

rough or splintered edges. Drill three access holes where indicated on the front section of the house by using the technique described for Basic Shape 1 (*see pages 20–21*), and then sand the cut edges smooth.

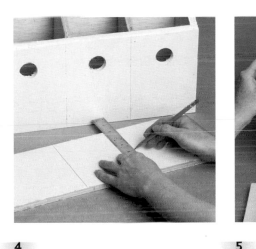

4

Using a ruler and a sharp pencil, mark dividing lines to act as your guide when applying the pink and yellow base colors. On the box front, mark a straight line 4¾ inches (12 cm) in from each side. For the lid, mark a line 5½ inches (14 cm) in from each side. Because this birdhouse is to be wall mounted, the back may be painted completely in either of the two colors since it will be hidden.

5

Apply a base coat of pink paint to the central section of the lid and to both end sections of the box. If you have a steady hand and a keen eye, you may do this freehand, following the pencil lines closely with your brush. Otherwise, apply a strip of masking tape next to the pencil line and simply paint up to it.

When the first coat is dry, apply a second in the same way. It is better to apply two thin coats than one thick coat. The masking tape can be peeled away when the second coat of paint is dry, leaving a straight, clean line.

6

Apply yellow paint to both ends of the lid section and to the central part of the main birdhouse shape. Again, masking-tape strips can be used to ensure that the paint lines are straight. When the paint on the side and front walls is dry, turn the box over and apply two coats of either yellow or pink paint to the back wall.

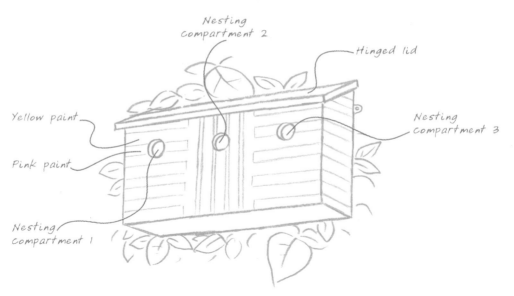

Nesting compartment 2

Hinged lid

Yellow paint

Nesting Compartment 3

Pink paint

Nesting Compartment 1

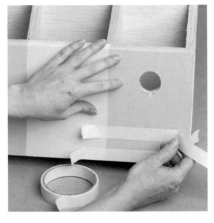

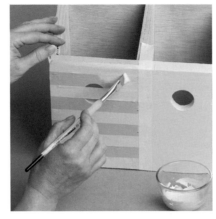

7

In order to create neat stripes, you need to use masking-tape strips again. Cut strips of masking tape and stick them in parallel horizontal bands across the pink sections at each end of the birdhouse. The strips should be approximately ¾ inch (2 cm) apart. You can do this by eye or measure the spacings more accurately using a ruler and pencil dots. When the horizontal bands are in place, stick two vertical bands to mask off the yellow central section.

8

Apply two coats of yellow paint to the unmasked areas at each end, using a smaller artist's paintbrush to completely minimize any overspill. Remember to allow the first coat to dry before applying the next. It is important to make sure that the edges of the tape are stuck down firmly before you begin, so the paint does not bleed underneath the tape, resulting in a ragged and uneven edge.

9

Stick strips of masking tape in parallel vertical bands on the central yellow section, leaving an approximately ¼-inch (6-mm) space between each one. Apply two coats of pink paint to the unmasked areas, allowing the first coat to dry before applying the next.

HINTS AND SUGGESTIONS

● *A perch may be added just under each of the entrance holes. See Basic Shape 3 on pages 24–25 for instructions.*

● *This birdhouse is designed for wall mounting; therefore, the house should be positioned at least 6–10 feet (1.8–3 meters) above ground level. This is to deter any squirrels, small rodents, or other predators from gaining access to the nesting compartments, where they can eat eggs or harm nestlings.*

● *You can also mount this birdhouse on a fence or on railings, however, using hanging brackets and wire (see main photo on page 31).*

BEACH CABANA BIRDS

This multicompartment birdhouse is ideal for purple martins. They are communal birds that usually make their homes in small cavities in trees. Your beach cabana will hopefully provide a home for three families, and because these birds like to return to the same nesting site each year, you will probably see the same feathery faces for quite a few years to come.

10

When all the paintwork is dry, remove the strips of masking tape, peeling each strip away slowly and carefully to reveal the contrast stripes beneath. If any bleeding has occurred and there are some ragged edges, retouch the paint using a fine artist's brush.

11

When all the tape strips have been removed, turn the box around and mark positions for the brass hanging brackets on each side, about 1 inch (2.5 cm) down from the top edge. Make a pilot hole at each pencil dot using the awl, replace the brackets into position, then screw them securely in place.

12

To complete the birdhouse, the lid must be securely attached with two hinges. Lay the house on its back with the lid, painted side down, next to it as shown. Position the hinges about 2 inches (5 cm) in from the lid edge and mark the screw holes on the lid and the angled top edge of the back section with pencil dots. Make a pilot hole at each pencil dot using the awl then screw the hinges securely into position.

Gingerbread Cottage

This one looks good enough to eat— let's hope the birds don't have the same opinion! Basic Shape 2 (*see page 22*) has simply been customized, with the addition of decorative scallops and a few architectural details to achieve the classic gingerbread cottage characteristics. We chose a rich ginger color paint for the main walls, and the roof was painted pink and white to resemble the frosting on a cake—with matching windows that look like iced cookies. The house is finished with a small section of dowel that looks like a white marshmallow atop the chimney!

You will need:

- basic tool kit (*see pages 8–11*)
- Basic Shape 2 template (*see page 156*), Gingerbread Cottage template (*see page 159*)
- plain paper for templates
- half sheet 1/2-in. (12-mm)-thick plywood— 2 x 2 ft (61 x 61 cm)
- approx. 6-in. (15-cm) square of 1/4-in. (6-mm)-thick plywood
- approx. 6-in. (15-cm) square of 2 x 2-in. (5- x 5-cm) lumber for chimney
- approx. 3/4-in. (2-cm) square of 1-in. (2.5-cm)-diameter dowel for chimney cap
- 3 x 1/2-in. (7.5 cm x 12-mm) ship lumber for door, or cut from the 1/2-in. (12-mm) plywood

- wood glue
- approx. seventy 1-in. (2.5-cm) paneling nails
- wood filler
- 40-oz. (1-l) can primer
- medium- and fine-grade sandpaper
- 40-oz. (1-l) cans of latex-based exterior-grade ginger-brown, pink, and white paint
- household and artist's paintbrushes
- two 11/2-in. (38-mm) brass flush hinges, plus fixing screws
- one 1-in. (2.5-cm) brass hanging bracket or turn button, plus fixing screws

First Steps | Trace and enlarge the Basic Shape 2 templates provided on page 156 to full size; then cut out the paper pattern pieces and transfer the outlines to a sheet of ¹/₂-inch (12-mm)-thick plywood. Mark any drill-hole positions with pencil dots. Carefully cut out the pieces using a jigsaw. Use a medium-grade sandpaper to smooth off any rough edges. Drill an access hole where indicated on the front section, using the technique described for

 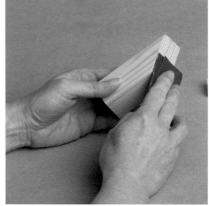 

1

Trace the shaped scallop templates on page 159 and carefully cut the paper. Transfer the outlines to a small sheet of ¹/₄-inch (6-mm)-thick plywood, then cut out each piece carefully using a jigsaw fitted with a fine blade suitable for cutting tight curves. This is a tricky operation, so it is handy to have some spare plywood in case you need to recut a piece or two. Sand the edges of each piece until smooth.

2

Use the miter saw to cut the door shape according to the template on page 159 from the 3-inch (7.5-cm)-wide strip (if using the ¹/₂-inch (12-mm)-thick plywood, use the jigsaw). The chimney stack is also cut using the miter saw from the 2-inch (5-cm)-square length of lumber. One end should be cut straight, the other end at a 45-degree angle.

The longest side of the chimney should measure 3 inches (7.5 cm). Sand all freshly cut edges smooth using a medium-grade sandpaper.

3

Glue the small square of thin plywood that forms the chimney top to the flat end of the chimney stack, making sure that the small overhang is equal on all four sides. Secure it in place with two paneling nails. Cut a ³/₄-inch (2-cm)-long piece of round dowel for the chimney cap, then sand both ends smooth. Glue the cap to the top of the chimney. Allow the glue to set completely.

Basic Shape 1 (*see page 20*), and sand the cut edges. Assemble Basic Shape 2 and secure the base access flap (*see pages 22 and 25*). Fill all joints and voids with wood filler; then sand smooth when dry. Wipe away dust particles; then apply the two coats of primer, sanding smooth with fine-grade sandpaper between coats.

NOTE

Use the jigsaw or a hacksaw to cut one chimney top, five windows, and the two roof pieces for the door from ¼-inch (6-mm)-thick plywood, using the templates on page 159.

4

Mark the position of the angled end of the chimney on the roof with pencil dots. Apply wood glue to the base of the chimney, then position it on the roof. Press firmly into position and wipe away any excess glue with a damp cloth. Allow the glue to set a little, then secure the chimney with two paneling nails.

5

Take the two small rectangular sections that will form the roof over the door. Glue the shorter of the two in place on the sloping left side of the door, matching the top edge with the apex of the door. Glue the longer roof section in place so that the top edge overlaps the first. Secure both sections with a paneling nail when the glue has set fully.

6

Apply a base coat of pink paint to the roof of the cottage and let dry. When the first coat is dry you may apply a second coat to ensure an even coverage and a solid color. While the paint on the roof is drying, paint the five thin plywood squares with the same color. These will form the windows on the sides and back of the cottage.

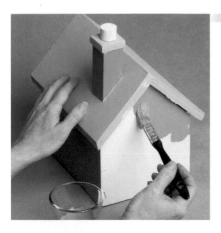

7

Apply two coats of the ginger-brown paint to the four cottage walls, the chimney, and the side edges of the door. A small household paintbrush can be used to paint the large areas, while a smaller artist's brush is more suitable for the chimney parts and door frame.

8

Check the scalloped pieces against the roof to ensure that they fit correctly. If they don't, adjust the shapes using sandpaper or trim with a hacksaw. Prime the four sections, and when dry, apply two coats of white paint. Paint the top chimney piece with white paint, too.

9

Use wood glue to fix the scallops in place, securing the side sections first, then applying the mitered section to the gables. Allow the glue to set a little; then secure the scallops, using a few paneling nails spaced at 2-inch (5-cm) intervals along the length. Be careful not to split the plywood when driving in the nails.

ORNAMENTAL GRASSES

Ornamental grasses are often neglected as a potential source of food for birds. Most grasses are low-maintenance and will yield a plentiful supply of seeds year after year. Choose plumed varieties such as pampas grass or fountain grass, and others that develop seed heads such as bluestem grass or feather reed grass. When the seeds are ripe, you can simply sit back and enjoy watching your garden visitors help themselves.

HINTS AND SUGGESTIONS

- *All painted architectural details and the scalloped edges can be used on Basic Shapes 3 and 4 (see pages 24–27) to achieve a similar effect. Simply alter the length of the scallops to fit the edges of the roof sections and adapt the size of the windows to be more in scale with the shape.*

- *You can use a cotton swab dipped in the pink paint to apply the pink spots, too. Simply dip the tip of a cotton swab in some pink paint, then dab it once firmly in position on the scallop to leave a nice round spot of color behind.*

- *For information on post mounting, see pages 18–19.*

10

Use a small artist's paintbrush and white paint to add the window frame and door frame details. You can do this freehand or mark out the position of the details more accurately with faint pencil lines and a ruler. The frame should be about ¼ inch (6 mm) wide.

11

Use wood glue to secure the door to the center of the front end of the cottage and the windows to the other three sides. Two windows are positioned on each side, while the remaining window goes in the center of the back wall. When the glue has set, secure the door and windows with a few paneling nails. Do not try to do this when the glue is wet because the pieces can slide out of place as you hammer.

12

Finally, take a small amount of pink paint on a palette or a small dish and, using a fine artist's brush, paint pink spots in the center of each of the rounded scallops.

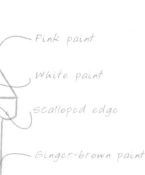

Entry to nesting compartment

Pink paint

White paint

Scalloped edge

Ginger-brown paint

Log Cabin

What bird could resist taking up residence in this log cabin? A real little house on the prairie, complete with polka-dot curtains, this birdhouse is made from Basic Shape 2 (*see page 22*), with dowels and half dowels tacked to the outside. Only simple cutting is involved, and since there are no complicated joints, the project can be completed quickly and neatly, even by a novice. The log cabin architecture is enhanced with dazzling paintwork, which can be adapted to create your own unique house.

You will need:

- basic tool kit (*see pages 8–11*)
- Basic Shape 2 template (*see page 156*), Log Cabin template (*see page 159*)
- plain paper for templates
- half sheet ½-in. (12-mm)-thick plywood —2 x 2 ft (61 x 61 cm)
- three 6-ft (2-m) lengths of ¾-in. (2-cm)-diameter pine doweling for roof
- three 6-ft (2-m) lengths of ¾-in. (2-cm) half dowel for walls
- approx. 2-ft (61-cm) length of ¼-in. (6-mm)-square beading for window frame
- approx. 1 in. (2.5 cm) of ¼-in. (6-mm)-diameter dowel for perch
- wood glue

- approx. fifty 1-in. (2.5-cm) paneling nails
- approx thirty 1-in. (2.5-cm) fine finishing nails
- wood filler
- 40-oz. (1-l) can primer
- medium-grade sandpaper
- 40-oz. (1-l) cans of blue, dark brown, and light brown wood stain
- 4-oz. (100-g) bottle black, red, and white artist's acrylic paint
- household and artist's paintbrushes
- two 1½-in. (38-mm) brass flush hinges, plus fixing screws
- one 1-in. (2.5-cm) brass hanging bracket or turn button, plus fixing screws

First Steps | Trace and enlarge the Basic Shape 2 templates provided on page 156 to full size (remember that this design uses the trimmed roof shape); then cut out the paper pattern pieces and transfer the outlines to a sheet of ½-inch (12-mm)-thick plywood, making sure to mark any drill-hole positions with pencil dots. Carefully cut out the pieces using a jigsaw, adjusting the baseplate to cut the outer edge of each roof

1

Paint the window details freehand on each side of the birdhouse. Use a small artist's paintbrush and white acrylic paint to completely fill in the window rectangle. This acts as a base for the colored details. Paint the background black and the curtains red. When dry, add some darker red paint to make the "folds" in the curtains, and add some white polka dots.

2

Cut all the dowels and half dowels to size. Starting with one side of the birdhouse, cut three lengths of half dowel to match the wall length exactly, then six more shorter lengths to fit at each side of the window. Duplicate these cuts for the other side of the house. Cut half dowels in the same way to fit the back. Use your miter saw to cut the angled pieces to fit the pitch of the roof.

For the door end, follow the same basic rules, cutting shorter pieces to fit each side of the doorway. For the roof, cut 14 lengths of dowel, each ½ inch (12 mm) longer than the roof. Sand all the cut edges smooth.

3

Fix the cut pieces into position on the house with wood glue and fine paneling nails. Work on one side at a time, gluing each section first, then hammering in a nail at each end of the piece to hold it securely. Complete both window sides of the house, then the back, and finally the front. Wipe away excess glue with a damp cloth; then allow the glue to dry completely. Remember to use an exterior-quality adhesive.

section at a 45-degree angle. Use a medium-grade sandpaper to smooth off any rough or splintered edges, especially along the 45-degree cut. Be aware that using a jigsaw at an angle can be tricky and sometimes leaves an untidy edge.

Assemble Basic Shape 2 (*see pages 22–23*) and secure the base access flap as described on page 24. Fill all joints and voids with wood filler, then sand smooth when dry.

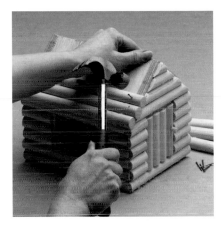

4

Cut four lengths of half-dowel to fit the door vertically. Use wood glue and fine paneling nails to hold the pieces in place. When the glue has dried, mark the position of the door handle with a pencil dot. Cut a 1-inch (2.5-cm) piece of ¼-inch (6-mm)-diameter pine dowel, then sand the ends smooth.

Using a drill bit to match the diameter of the dowel, drill a hole at the marked position. Squeeze a drop of wood glue onto one end of the dowel, then push it gently into the drill hole.

5

Using a fine drill bit, make a small pilot hole in each of the roofing dowels—1 inch (2.5 cm) from each end. Each hole must run vertically through the center of the dowel so it will lie straight and level when attached to the roof of the cabin. The pilot hole will prevent the dowel from splitting when the nail is driven through. Make sure the drill bit has a slightly smaller diameter than the nail or screw to be used.

6

Take one of the roofing dowels and place a paneling nail in each of the pilot holes. Tap each nearly all the way through with your hammer, so that the tip of the nail protrudes on the other side.

Apply a fine line of wood glue to the underside of the dowel and position it along the lower edge of the cabin roof. Tilt the cabin a little so the dowel is balanced and in no danger of rolling away, then hammer both nails in, securing the dowel in position. Attach the remaining pieces in the same way.

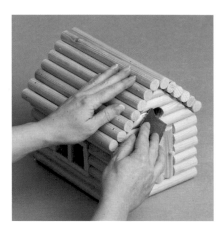

7

Use a small hacksaw to cut the length of ½-inch (12-mm)-square beading to fit the windows on both sides of the cabin. Begin with the top and lower frame, then add the side and central pieces. Sand the cut edges and check that they fit snugly. Do this for the windows on both sides of the log cabin. ·

8

Apply a thin bead of wood glue to one side of each beading piece and stick it firmly in place around the window. Use a damp cotton swab to wipe away any glue that seeps out during this process. Allow the glue to set a little then use a fine finishing nail at both ends of each piece to secure it to the cabin wall. Be careful not to split the molding as you nail.

9

When all the glue has set completely, drill the entrance hole in the front of the cabin. Refer to the paper template on page 159 for positioning, and mark the center of the hole with a pencil dot. Make a small pilot hole at the dot using an awl; then drill a larger hole using a spade bit. Sand smooth any rough or splintered edges.

Entry to nesting compartment

Dark brown wood stain

Blue wood stain

Light brown wood stain

Door handle perch

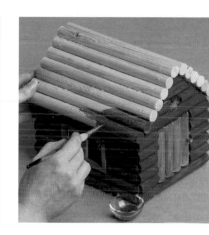

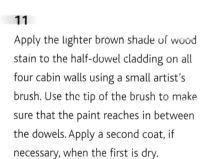

10

Pour a small amount of blue wood stain into a dish and use an artist's paintbrush to apply the stain to the front door and the window frames. Apply a second coat if the effect is patchy. Allow the second coat to dry.

11

Apply the lighter brown shade of wood stain to the half-dowel cladding on all four cabin walls using a small artist's brush. Use the tip of the brush to make sure that the paint reaches in between the dowels. Apply a second coat, if necessary, when the first is dry.

12

Apply at least one or two coats of dark brown wood stain to the roof of the log cabin. It is best to use a small artist's brush for this so you are able to reach all the surface areas of the round dowels.

CARING FOR INJURED BIRDS

Bird-watchers and nature lovers often find casualties. Tiny fledglings can fall from a nest or be attacked and injured by rodents or a cat. Window collisions often result in a dazed-and-confused bird unable to fend for itself. Don't rush to the injured bird's aid immediately—watch and wait, the creature may just need a little time to rest and recover by itself. If there is no improvement, put on some gloves and gently lift the bird; then place it in a dark, well-ventilated box. Take the bird as soon as possible to a wildlife center where professionals can give the appropriate treatment and care.

Church

The inspiration for this little country church, both in form and color, comes from New England. This one has faux clapboard siding drawn by hand with a waterproof marker—the birds won't know the difference. The tower even has a tiny clock made from a small jar lid.

You will need:

- basic tool kit
  (*see pages 8–11*)

- Basic Shape 2 template
  (*see page 156*), Church
  template (*see page 160*)

- plain paper for templates

- half sheet ½-in. (12-mm)-
  thick plywood—2 x 2 ft
  (61 x 61 cm)

- one sheet ¼-in. (6-mm)-
  thick plywood—2 x 4 ft
  (61 x 122 cm)

- 2 x 1-in. (5 x 2.5-cm)
  length of lumber for
  clock tower and door

- wood glue

- approx. fifty 1-in.
  (2.5-cm) paneling nails

- wood filler

- 40-oz. (1-l) can primer

- medium- and fine-grade
  sandpaper

- 40-oz. (1-l) cans dark gray
  and blue-gray latex-based
  exterior grade paint

- black waterproof marker

- small screw-top-jar lid

- two small wood screws to
  attach to the clock face

- two No. 8, 2-in.
  (4 x 50-mm) chrome
  domed slothead wood
  screws to attach the door
  in place and as handles

- household and artist's
  paintbrushes

- two 1½-in. (38-mm)
  brass flush hinges, plus
  fixing screws

- one 1-in. (2.5-cm) brass
  hanging bracket, plus
  fixing screws

First Steps | Trace and enlarge the Basic Shape 2 templates provided on page 156 to full size; then cut out the paper pattern pieces and transfer the outlines to a sheet of ½-inch (12-mm)-thick, and ¼-inch (6-mm)-thick plywood as directed. Be sure to mark any drill-hole positions with pencil dots. Carefully cut out the pieces using a jigsaw. Use a medium-grade sandpaper to smooth any rough or splintered edges. Drill an access hole

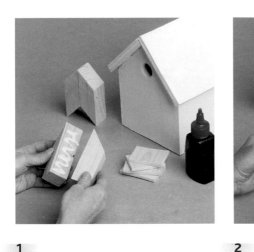

1

Lay the templates for the door and the tower pieces onto the 2 x 1-inch (5 x 2.5-cm) lumber and trace along the 45-degree sloping edges to form guidelines for cutting. Cut out the pieces with a miter saw; then sand the cut edges smooth.

The tower pieces have two angled edges, while the door pieces each have one angled edge and one straight cut edge. Glue the pieces together in pairs as shown above to form the door and tower.

2

Take the two small rectangular roof sections and glue them to the top of the tower and to the top of the door. Secure the shorter piece first; then position the longer section so it overlaps neatly at the apex. Allow the glue to set a little; then use one or two paneling nails to secure each piece in position. Do not try to do this when the glue is wet because the pieces will slide out of place.

3

Place the tower on the roof and mark its position with a faint pencil line. Apply glue to the roof within the pencil guidelines and press the tower section in place. Wipe away any excess glue with a damp cloth. Once the glue has set a little, secure the tower by hammering a few paneling nails at an angle through the lower pointed edges and into the roof on both sides.

where indicated on the front section using the technique described for Basic Shape 1 (*see page 20*), and sand the cut edges smooth. Assemble Basic Shape 2 (*see pages 22–23*) and secure the base access flap as described on page 24. Fill all joints and voids with wood filler, then sand smooth when dry. Wipe away any dust particles with a damp cloth. Apply two coats of primer, sanding the house smooth using a fine-grade sandpaper between coats.

4

Apply a coat of primer to the door and clock tower. When the primer is dry, apply the first coat of dark gray paint to the rooftop of the main church building, the clock tower, and door. The dark color may appear patchy after the first coat, so apply a second coat, if necessary, when the first is completely dry.

5

Take the precut window pieces and apply a coat of primer to the fronts and all of the edges. When the primer is dry, apply two coats of dark gray paint, allowing the first to dry before applying the second. Similarly, prime the surface of the small metal screw top that will become the clock face. When it is dry, apply two coats of gray paint.

6

When the gray paint is dry, apply a coat of blue-gray to the remaining surfaces, including the doorway, the clock tower, and the overhanging eaves under the roof edges. Allow the first coat to dry completely, then apply a second coat, if necessary.

7

When the blue-gray topcoat is dry, apply the faux clapboard lines. Use a ruler and a pencil to mark horizontal parallel lines at about ½-inch (12-mm) intervals on all four sides of the church, plus the sides of the door and the tower. Follow these pencil lines with black permanent marker, but do not use a ruler. Wobbly lines add to the rustic effect!

8

Arrange four window pieces in an evenly spaced row on one side wall and mark the position of the lower corners of each with a pencil dot. Apply a little glue to the back of each piece then press the windows firmly into place using the pencil dots as a guide. When the glue has set, secure each piece in place with a few paneling nails. Fix four windows on the other side and two on the back.

9

Because the door is quite chunky, it will require more than wood glue to hold it in place securely. Use an awl to make two small pilot holes where the door handles will be. Place the door in position, then drill two holes through the door and into the front wall of the church.

SEASONAL PLANTING TO ATTRACT BIRDS

When considering what to plant in your garden to attract birds, look at varieties that will flower throughout the seasons and develop seeds or fruits at different times. You will not only benefit from a consistently beautiful garden, but you will also have a host of birds to watch at your leisure during the warmer months.

HINTS AND SUGGESTIONS

- *Architectural features, such as the clock tower and door, can also be added to Basic Shapes 3 and 4 to create a different church shape. The color scheme may also be changed to suit your own taste or planting scheme.*

- *Drill a large hole using a spade bit through the center of the tower where the clock face is located and hang a tiny bell in it. This will tinkle lightly in the breeze.*

10

Apply wood glue to the back of the door, then press it firmly into position on the front wall of the church. Wipe away any excess glue with a damp cloth. When the glue has set, drive a long roundheaded wood screw into each pilot hole, securing the door in place and providing some faux door handles.

11

Mark the center of the clock face with a pencil dot. Make a hole through the metal using the point of your awl—check that the hole is large enough to accommodate a small fixing screw. Use a fine artist's brush and a little blue paint to add a pair of hands and some dots to indicate the numbers on the clock face.

12

When the painted details on the clock face are dry, secure it in position on the front of the clock tower. Hold the face in the correct position and place the point of the awl though the hole in the center to make a pilot hole for the screw in the tower beneath. Drive in the fixing screw to secure the clock face.

Nesting compartment

Clock face

Gray paint

Door with handles

Windows— gray paint

Blue-gray paint

Cinderella's Castle

Any little girl (or adult) with a romantic streak will adore this fairy-tale castle, a classic pink confection complete with turrets and shiny silver rooftops. Not only is this birdhouse a delightful addition to your backyard, but it also provides an opportunity for a little recycling—the turrets are made from old plastic dish-soap bottles and the rooftops are trimmed plastic funnels.

You will need:

- basic tool kit
  (*see pages 8–11*)
- Basic Shape 2 template
  (*see page 156*), Cinderella's
  Castle template
  (*see page 160*)
- plain paper for templates
- half sheet ½-in. (12-mm)-
  thick plywood—2 x 2 ft
  (61 x 61 cm)
- half sheet ¼-in. (6-mm)-
  thick plywood—2 x 2 ft
  (61 x 61 cm)
- four empty plastic
  dish-soap bottles
- four 3¾-in. (9.5-cm)
  small plastic funnels
- approx. 12-in. (30.5-cm)
  length of ½ x ½-in.
  (12 x 12-mm)-square
  dowel for tower supports
- wood glue
- approx. fifty 1-in.
  (2.5-cm) paneling nails
- approx. thirty
  1-in. (2.5-cm)
  fine finishing nails
- eight No. 6 ½-in.
  (3.5 x 12-mm)
  brass roundhead
  wood screws

- wood filler
- 40-oz. (1-l) can primer
- medium and fine-grade
  sandpaper
- waterproof thick
  black marker
- one can each of
  metallic silver and
  pink spray paint
- artist's paintbrush
- two 1½-in. (38-mm)
  brass flush hinges, plus
  fixing screws
- one 1-in. (2.5-cm) brass
  hanging bracket or turn
  button, plus fixing screws

First Steps | Trace and enlarge the templates for Basic Shape 2, provided on page 156, and the Cinderella's Castle templates, given on page 160, to full size; then cut out the paper pattern pieces. Transfer the outlines to the sheets of plywood as directed on the templates, making sure to mark any drill-hole positions with pencil dots. Carefully cut out the pieces using a jigsaw. Use a medium-grade sandpaper to smooth any rough or

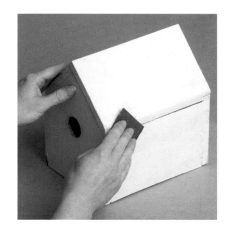

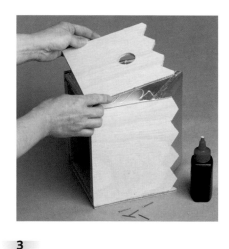

1

Assemble Basic Shape 2 (*see pages 22–23*) and secure the base access flap as described on page 24. Fill all joints and voids with wood filler and sand smooth when dry. After wiping away any dust particles with a damp cloth, apply the first coat of primer to the bare wooden surfaces. When the first coat is dry, sand it smooth using a fine-grade sandpaper; then apply a second coat of primer.

2

Stand the primed box on a large sheet of newspaper and apply two thin coats of metallic silver spray paint to the roof only. The edges of the roof may be difficult to reach when the shaped outer walls are added to the basic shape. This paint can be retouched at a later stage. Do the spraying outside or in a well-ventilated room.

3

Apply a generous amount of wood glue to each castle battlement side; then press the shaped side sections into position. Wipe away any excess glue from the edges with a damp cloth. When the glue has set a little, fix the sides in place securely with paneling nails. Glue and nail the back and front sections in place. Take care to correctly align the predrilled entrance holes. Fill any gaps with wood filler, then sand smooth when dry.

splintered edges, especially along the 45-degree-angle cut. Using the jigsaw at an angle can be tricky and sometimes leaves an untidy edge. Drill access holes in the main front section and the shaped front section where indicated using the technique described for Basic Shape 1 (*see page 20*), then sand the edges smooth and wipe away any dust particles with a damp cloth.

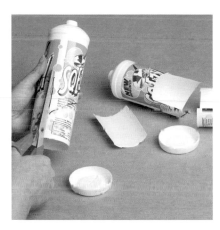

4

Wipe away any dust particles with a damp cloth; then apply the first coat of primer to the bare wooden surfaces. When the first coat is dry, sand the house smooth with a fine-grade sandpaper; then apply a second coat of primer. Examine the surface finish at this stage, and if it still looks a little rough, resand before applying a third coat of primer. The spray paint topcoat tends to accentuate any surface irregularities.

5

Pick up the ½ x ½-inch (12 x 12-mm)-square dowel and cut eight short tower supports using the miter saw. These pieces should be straight at one end and cut to a 45-degree angle at the other. The longest edge of each piece should measure approximately 1½ inches (4 cm).

Glue two supports to each corner of the birdhouse as shown above, making sure that the longest side of the support lies next to the corner of the birdhouse. When the glue has set a little and the supports are held in place, drive two paneling nails into each one.

6

Cut off the base of each plastic bottle and wrap the semicircular template along the cut edge. Mark the outline using a waterproof marker. Cut along the marked line to achieve the lower sloping edge of the tower. Place the rectangular template along the lower cut edge of the bottle and mark it. Cut away this section. The rectangular cutout allows the tower to be placed easily onto the corner of the birdhouse.

7

Apply two coats of pink spray paint to the birdhouse and the plastic towers, allowing the first coat to dry before applying the next. Examine the paint finish after the second coat and apply a third, if necessary. If the pink spray paint spreads onto the previously painted silver rooftop, it can be retouched later.

8

Place the plastic towers onto each corner of the castle. The rectangular cutaway area should fit neatly over the corner, and the pointed lower edges should reach down just beyond the tower supports. Nail the tower to each support with a finishing nail. When the towers are supported, drill a small hole into each support and drive in a short roundhead screw to hold the tower more securely.

9

Neatly trim the vertical edge of each plastic funnel away with scissors and use a small hacksaw to remove the narrow tube at the top. The plastic is thin and should be easy to cut and shape. You will be left with four cone shapes. Sand any ragged or uneven edges smooth using a fine-grade sandpaper. Wipe away any dust particles with a damp cloth to prepare for the metallic silver topcoat.

Metallic silver spray paint

Tower tops made from funnels

Pink spray paint

Entry to nesting compartment

SHRUBS AND TREES FOR SHELTER AND ROOSTING

As the colder months approach, you may see some of your garden visitors migrate to warmer climates. Those that are left behind, however, will need safe roosting and perching places away from wind, rain, and snow. Plant evergreen shrubs and trees, or coniferous varieties that have dense foliage throughout the year. The birds will be grateful to nestle in a warm place away from inclement weather conditions.

10

Place the four cones onto a sheet of newspaper—either outside or in a well-ventilated room—and apply one or two thin coats of metallic silver spray paint. Always allow the first coat to dry before applying the second. The metallic finish works extremely well on the smooth plastic surface. Set the cones aside to dry completely.

11

Apply a generous amount of glue (wood or a specialty plastic glue) to the top of each tower; then place a silver cone on top. While the glue is still wet, you can alter the position of the cone so that the hole at the top aligns perfectly with the hole at the top of the bottle/tower. Allow the glue to dry completely before moving the castle. Wipe away excess glue with a damp cloth.

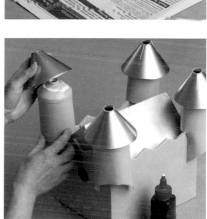

12

Wrap the window template around each tower. Using a sharp pencil, trace the small rectangular shapes that will form the windows onto each tower and fill in each one with silver metallic paint. Paint three windows on each side of the castle. Trace the shape of the door, using the template provided, on the front of the castle and paint it silver. Allow all of the decorative paint to dry before mounting the castle on a sturdy pole or post.

HINTS AND SUGGESTIONS

• *Pink is a classic color for a fairy-tale castle but any pastel color would be just as effective. Choose one to match the color scheme of your exterior or the flowers in the backyard.*

• *This birdhouse can also be hung from a tree. Insert a brass screw eye into the front and back sections—close to the roof apex at each end. Suspend the house with strong cords tied securely to the eyes.*

Haunted House

This sinister variation on Basic Shape 3 (*see page 157*) retains the tall, two-story height, but the silhouette changes slightly and a small tower is added to the roof to increase the spookiness. However, the birds will not be daunted by the dark and eerie exterior, since the house is still cozy inside.

You will need:

- basic tool kit (*see pages 8–11*)
- Basic Shape 3 template (*see page 157*), Haunted House template (*see page 161*)
- plain paper for templates
- one sheet ½-in. (12-mm)-thick plywood—2 x 4 ft (61 x 122 cm)
- one sheet ¼-in. (6-mm)-thick plywood—2 x 4 ft (61 x 122 cm)
- approx. 6 in. (15 cm) of 2 x 2-in. (5 x 5-cm) lumber for chimney
- wood glue
- approx. fifty 1-in. (2.5-cm) paneling nails
- wood filler
- 40-oz. (1-l) can primer
- coarse-, medium-, and fine-grade sandpaper
- waterproof black marker
- 40-oz. (1-l) cans latex-based exterior-grade black and yellow paint
- household and artist's paintbrushes
- two 1½-in. (38-mm) brass flush hinges, plus fixing screws
- one 1-in. (2.5-cm) brass turn button, plus fixing screw

First Steps | Trace and enlarge the templates provided on page 161 to full size; then cut out the paper pattern pieces and transfer the outlines to a sheet of ½-inch (12-mm)- thick plywood, and ¼-inch (6-mm)-thick plywood as directed. Make sure to mark any drill-hole positions with pencil dots, and include any other decorative details such as windows and doors, and construction guidelines for the floor. Carefully cut out the pieces using a jigsaw;

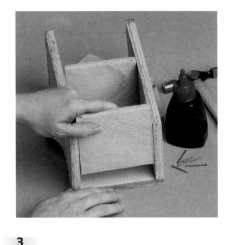

1

Lay the front section facedown on your work surface and glue both side pieces to it. After ensuring that the pieces are aligned correctly, allow the glue to set a little. When the side pieces seem to be held firmly, flip the shape over and insert paneling nails at 2-inch (5-cm) intervals to hold the sides securely. Wipe away any glue that may seep out of the joints with a damp cloth.

2

This birdhouse has two interior chambers to accommodate two bird families, so a division must be inserted. Slot the square floor section between the walls using the pencil lines as a guide. If it does not fit, use a coarse-grade sandpaper to adjust the size. However, if it is too small, you will need to cut a new piece. Apply a bead of wood glue to three sides, then slot the floor into position. When the glue is set, use paneling nails to hold it in place.

3

Secure the base section in place using the same method. Apply plenty of wood glue, and use at least three paneling nails along each side to make sure that it is held securely in place. Wipe away any glue that has seeped out with a damp cloth.

then use a medium-grade sandpaper to smooth any rough or splintered edges. Drill two access holes where indicated in the front section using the technique described in Basic Shape 1 (*see page 20*), and sand the cut edges smooth.

NOTE

Pay extra attention to the curved edge of the access door in the back section of the birdhouse—this should be smooth and allow the door to open and close with ease.

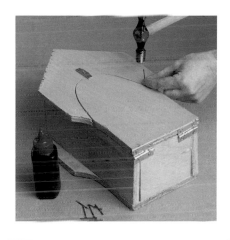

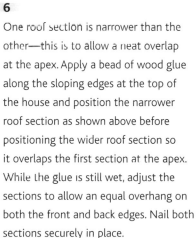

4

Lay the birdhouse on its front and squeeze a bead of wood glue about halfway down both of the side edges. You will see that the back section has been modified and is in two pieces. The upper piece will be fixed in place, while the lower section will be hinged and used as an access door.

Place both pieces in position so they align correctly with each other. Nail the upper part of the back to the sides; then screw a turn button to the top of the access doorway. Screw two brass hinges to the lower edge of the door and box to allow the access flap to open and close.

5

Take a rectangular upper side wall section and apply a bead of glue to both side edges. Slot in place as shown. The fit should be quite snug, so tap the piece in using a hammer, if necessary. Insert a few paneling nails to hold the section in place securely. Attach the remaining side wall in the same way.

6

One roof section is narrower than the other—this is to allow a neat overlap at the apex. Apply a bead of wood glue along the sloping edges at the top of the house and position the narrower roof section as shown above before positioning the wider roof section so it overlaps the first section at the apex. While the glue is still wet, adjust the sections to allow an equal overhang on both the front and back edges. Nail both sections securely in place.

HINTS AND SUGGESTIONS

• *The Haunted House may be slightly altered to hang on a wall. Both roof sections should be positioned so that the back edges lie flush with the back of the house. Two brass hanging brackets can be securely screwed to the house for attachment to a wall.*

• *Any of the Basic Shapes can be given the Haunted House treatment. Trace some windows on the front and side sections of the templates and paint them yellow; then paint the rest of the house with a few coats of matte black paint.*

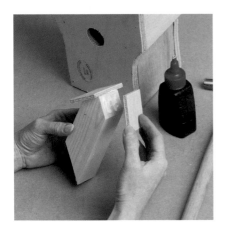

7

Take a 2 x 2-inch (5 x 5-cm)-square piece of wood and place the tower template along one face. Trace the outline and use the miter saw to cut the tower shape. Glue and nail the smaller roof section to the left slope at the top of the tower; then secure the section on the right side in the same way. The pieces should overlap neatly at the apex.

8

Apply wood glue to the sloping base of the tower and position on the right roof section as shown above. While the glue is still wet, you may adjust the position a little. Allow the glue to set and then secure the tower to the roof using two paneling nails.

9

Fill all joints and voids with wood filler, then sand smooth when dry. Wipe away any dust particles with a damp cloth before applying the first coat of primer to all of the bare wooden surfaces. When the first coat is dry, sand it smooth using a fine-grade sandpaper, then apply a second coat.

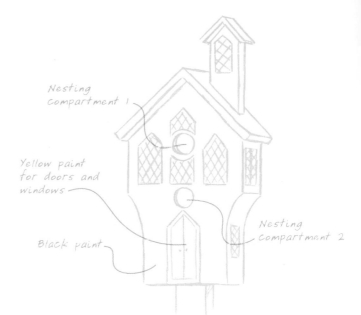

Nesting compartment 1

Yellow paint for doors and windows

Black paint

Nesting compartment 2

10

Trace the outlines of the windows and door using a pencil and ruler. Be sure to include the diamond-shaped pattern of small panes and the bolder lines that surround the door. Apply a coat of yellow paint over the pencil lines. You will be able to see the lines through the paint.

11

Use a thick waterproof marker to trace over all of pencil lines. Begin at the top of the house and work down so you won't smudge any of the black lines. Allow the lines to dry completely.

12

When the marker is dry, apply at least two coats of black paint to the entire birdhouse, painting carefully around the windows and doors. Allow each coat to dry before applying subsequent layers. The first two coats may appear very patchy—a solid coverage will be achieved after the third or fourth coat.

Swiss Chalet

Two tones of fresh spring green can transform Basic Shape 4 (*see page 157*) into a pretty chalet-style dwelling for your feathered visitors. This house even has its own yard, complete with a picket fence. The fence posts are simply plastic plant markers trimmed to size, then glued and pinned in place—you could use wooden popsicle sticks as an alternative.

You will need:

- basic tool kit (*see pages 8–11*)
- Basic Shape 4 template (*see page 157*), Swiss Chalet template (*see page 162*)
- plain paper for templates
- one sheet ½-in. (12-mm)-thick plywood—2 x 4 ft (61 x 122 cm)
- one sheet ¼-in. (6-mm)-thick plywood—2 x 4 ft (61 x 122 cm)
- one 1³⁄₈ x ½-in. (35 x 12-mm) length of wooden strip for the yard
- one pack of plastic garden plant markers
- wood glue
- approx. fifty 1-in. (2.5-cm) paneling nails
- approx. eighty fine veneer nails
- eight No. 6 1½-in. (3.5 x 40-mm) wood screws
- wood filler
- 40-oz. (1-l) can primer
- medium- and fine-grade sandpaper
- two shades of green paint, lilac, and white latex-based exterior-grade paint—40-oz. (1-l) cans
- household and artist's paintbrushes
- two 1½-in. (38-mm) brass flush hinges, plus fixing screws
- one 1-in. (2.5-cm) brass hanging bracket or turn button, plus fixing screws

First Steps | Trace and enlarge the Basic Shape 4 templates provided on page 157 to full size; then cut out the paper pattern pieces and transfer the outlines as directed to a sheet of $1/2$-inch (12-mm)-thick plywood, making sure to mark any drill-hole positions with pencil dots. Carefully cut out the pieces using a jigsaw. Use a medium-grade sandpaper to smooth any rough or splintered edges. Drill an access hole where

1

Assemble Basic Shape 4 (*see pages 26–27*) and secure the base access flap as described on page 24. Fill all joints and voids with wood filler and sand smooth when dry. Apply two coats of primer, sanding in between coats with a fine-grade sandpaper.

Use the template provided on page 162 to trace the outline of the door on the $1^3/8$ x $1/2$-inch (35 x 12-mm) strip. Carefully cut the shape using the miter saw. Glue and nail both roof sections to the door as shown above; then add a coat of primer.

2

Apply a coat of the darker green paint to the roof with a small household paintbrush. Allow the first coat to dry and examine the finish. If it looks a little patchy, apply a second coat. It is always better to paint two thin coats than one thick one.

3

Use the lighter shade of green paint for the main body of the birdhouse. Apply one thin coat, and after this has dried apply a second coat, if necessary. Remember to paint the underside of the roof overhang. You may require a smaller paintbrush for this job.

indicated on the front section using the technique described for Basic Shape 1 (*see page 20*), and sand the cut edges smooth. Trace the small templates for the door, roof, windows, and shutters given on page 162—these shapes are actual size and do not need to be enlarged. Care must be taken when cutting these small shapes because they can be difficult to handle.

4

Now for the architectural details. Use a small hacksaw to cut the two windows and four shutters from thin pieces of strip wood following the templates provided on page 162, then sand all the cut edges smooth. Apply a coat of white paint to both windows, and when dry add a frame of green using an artist's paintbrush as shown above. Paint the four shutters with lilac paint.

5

Paint the front door to match the shutters. Trace the small heart-shaped templates and copy the shape to the center of the door and to all four shutters. Using a small artist's paintbrush, carefully fill in the shapes using the darker shade of green paint, then allow to dry.

6

Apply a small amount of glue to the back of each shutter, and position one on each side of the windows, allowing a little of the green frame to show along the inner edge. The glue will be sufficient to hold these details in place until the next stage.

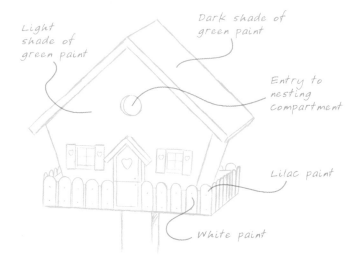

Light shade of green paint

Dark shade of green paint

Entry to nesting compartment

Lilac paint

White paint

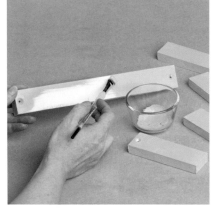

7

Use wood glue to secure the door to the front of the birdhouse in a central position, making sure that the lower edge aligns with the lower edge of the house. Glue the windows to the house on both sides of the door. When the glue has set, you may use a few fine veneer paneling nails to hold the windows and shutters in place and a few longer nails to secure the door in its position.

8

The base for the picket fence is made from four lengths of wood secured to the lower edge of the house. Using a hacksaw, cut the lengths as follows:
back: cut one 10½ inches (26.7 cm)
sides: cut two 6 inches (15.25 cm)
front: cut two 4¼ inches (11.5 cm)

Sand all cut edges smooth, apply a coat of primer to each one, and when dry apply one or two coats of the darker green paint.

9

Glue the front walls to the house on both sides of the front door as shown above, and when the glue has set, nail securely in place. Flip the house over and do the same with the longest remaining piece—make sure that it is placed centrally along the lower back edge. Wipe away any excess glue with a damp cloth.

CREATING A ROOSTING AREA

This birdhouse can be altered slightly to provide a perfect roosting spot. As the evening approaches you will notice that the birds will begin to head for a sheltered place in which to rest for the night. Many huddle together in tree branches for warmth and protection. To modify the chalet birdhouse, simply omit the entrance hole and the base flap; then drill a large hole through the center of the front and back sections about 2 inches (5 cm) from the lower edge. Pass a length of wooden dowel through both holes to form a perch both at the front and the back and a roosting perch inside.

HINTS AND SUGGESTIONS

The yard in this project can easily be added to Basic Shapes 1, 2, and 3. Simply cut the strips that form the walls slightly smaller to fit the perimeter and secure them to the body of the birdhouse, then apply the picket fence pieces in the same way.

10

Glue the side pieces to the perimeter between the front and the back strips. When the glue has set completely, mark and drill a pilot hole through the end of the front and back strips down into the sides. Countersink the drill hole; then drive a long wood screw into each strip to hold the pieces securely.

11

Trim the white plastic garden markers to a length of approximately 2 inches (5 cm) each. You will need 35 to 40 markers depending on the size. Sand all the cut edges smooth. Paint half of the markers lilac and leave the other half white. You can also use wooden plant sticks or popsicle sticks and paint half of them white.

12

Glue the fence pieces to the garden wall at intervals of approximately ¼ inch (6 mm). You do not need to measure this accurately—simply do it by eye. Alternate the colors, beginning with a white piece on both sides of the door. While the glue is still wet, you can alter the spacing until it looks balanced. Once the glue has set, secure each piece to the strip by using two small veneer nails.

Neoclassical Temple

The Ancient Greeks knew a thing or two about architecture. This mini-Parthenon birdhouse pays homage to that golden era of building design. The simple rectangular area in the center is surrounded by tall, elegant columns—any bird family will appreciate living in such an impressive home.

You will need:

- basic tool kit
  (*see pages 8–11*)

- Neoclassical Temple
  template (*see page 163*)

- plain paper for templates

- one sheet ¹/₂-in. (12-mm)-
  thick plywood—2 x 4 ft
  (61 x 122 cm)

- one sheet ¹/₄-in. (6-mm)-
  thick plywood—2 x 4 ft
  (61 x 122 cm)

- three 6 ft 6-in. (2.2-m)
  lengths of 1¹/₈-in.
  (28.5-mm)-diameter
  grooved dowel for
  columns

- 6 ft 6-in. (2.2-m) length
  of 1³/₈ x ¹/₈-in.
  (35 mm x 3-mm) strip
  wood for column bases

- 6 ft 6-in. (2.2-m) length
  of 1 x ¹/₂-in.
  (2.5 cm x 15-mm) strip
  wood for the frieze

- wood glue

- approx. fifty 1-in. (2.5-cm)
  paneling nails

- wood filler

- 40-oz. (1-l) can primer

- twenty-eight No. 6
  1¹/₂-in. (3.5 x 40-mm)-
  long wood screws

- fine-grade sandpaper

- 40-oz. (1-l) can latex-
  based exterior-grade
  brilliant white paint

- household paintbrush

- two 1¹/₂-in. (38-mm)
  brass flush hinges,
  plus fixing screws

- one 1-in. (2.5-cm) brass
  hanging bracket or turn
  button, plus fixing screws

First Steps | Trace and enlarge the templates provided on page 163 to full size; then cut out the paper pattern pieces and transfer the outlines to sheets of ½-inch (12-mm), and ¼-inch (6-mm)-thick plywood according to the template directions, making sure to mark all of the drill-hole positions with pencil dots. Drill an access hole where indicated on the front section using a spade bit

1

Glue and nail the sides of the central compartment to the back and front, as shown above, to make a rectangular box. Wipe away any glue that may have seeped out, then allow the glue to set completely. When the glue is dry, apply wood filler to the joints at each of the four corners and to any voids along the edges. When the filler is dry, sand the surface smooth to prepare for the primer and finishing topcoats.

2

Turn the box upside down and apply a bead of wood glue to the edges of the four walls. Place the base on top and press down firmly onto the glue, taking care to match the edges of the box with the edges of the cutout section in the base.

When the glue has set a little, hammer in a few paneling nails to hold the box securely to the base section. Use one at each corner and then at 2-inch (5-cm) intervals. As an alternative, you could use wood screws. Turn the box the right side up and wipe away any excess glue with a damp cloth.

3

Take one of the ¼-inch (6-mm)-thick plywood rectangular top sections and a 1 x ½-inch (2.5 x 12-mm)-length of strip wood. Using a miter saw or a small hacksaw, cut two lengths to fit across each short end of the plywood rectangle. Glue the strips in place, then cut another two lengths to fit snugly between them along the two longer side edges. Glue these in place in the same way. These strips form the frieze section of the roof.

When the glue has set a little, flip the shape over and secure the strips in place using paneling nails at 2-inch (5-cm) intervals.

centered on a pilot hole and drilling over a piece of square lumber (*see page 20*). Sand any cut, rough, or splintered edges smooth using fine-grade sandpaper, then wipe away any dust particles using a damp cloth.

> **NOTE**
>
> *It is essential that all of the drill-hole positions are marked accurately and clearly and the columns and bases are spaced evenly to ensure that the design is neat and symmetrical when completed. It is worth taking your time at this stage for a successful end result.*

4

Using the miter saw, cut twenty-eight 1³⁄₈-inch (35-mm) squares from the length of strip wood. These small squares will form the bases and tops for each of the columns. Sand the cut edges of each square smooth. After referring to the pattern template on page 163, glue each square in place around the box base and on the underside of the roof section as shown above. You will need to place the squares accurately so they correspond with the columns at the top and bottom when the birdhouse is fully assembled.

5

Using the miter saw, cut fourteen 6¹⁄₂-inch (16.5-cm)-long pieces from the lengths of grooved dowel. Take the time to measure and cut each one accurately—it is worth it to achieve a good result. Sand the cut ends of each column to remove any splinters.

Apply a coat of primer to each column and to the central box, the base, and the roof section. When the first coat is dry, sand it smooth using a fine-grade sandpaper before applying a second coat of primer and a topcoat of brilliant white.

6

Use wood glue to secure a column to each of the square bases as shown above. Make sure that the columns are placed accurately in the center of each square. Press each column down firmly onto the glue; then use a damp cloth to wipe away any excess. Allow the glue to set enough to hold the columns firmly, then flip the shape over.

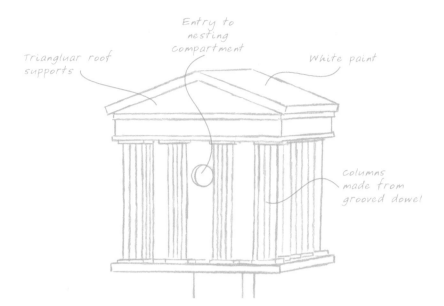

Entry to nesting compartment

Triangluar roof supports

White paint

Columns made from grooved dowel

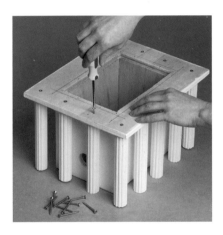

7

Use an electric drill to make a pilot hole through the base and down into the center of each column. Be sure to use a drill bit that matches the diameter of the screw. Drive a screw into each pilot hole—securing each column to the base. While the shape is upside down, take this opportunity to attach the base flap. Use two brass hinges and a brass hanging bracket to hold it in the closed position, as described on pages 22–23.

8

Turn the shape right-side up and squeeze some wood glue onto the top of each column. Place the roof section on top, matching up all the squares with the column tops. This stage of assembly may be a little tricky, but if you take your time you will not experience problems. Beginning at the front, make sure that the columns are in position; then drill pilot holes through the roof section and down the center of each of the four columns.

9

Insert a screw into each of the four pilot holes to secure the columns in position. Wipe away any excess glue with a damp cloth. Turn the shape around and repeat the process for the four columns along the back edge. Next secure the three columns along each side in the same way. This will ensure that all the columns are standing straight and parallel to each other.

HINTS AND SUGGESTIONS

• *Although this style of building is classically white in color, you could add a modern, quirky twist and paint it any color you like. How about a pink Parthenon or maybe a slick metallic finish?*

• *This birdhouse is heavy, so be sure to mount it securely on a sturdy post using heavy-duty screws.*

• *The grooved columns add a special touch to this design, but if you have difficulty locating them, use plain ones instead.*

10

When the glue is dry, attach the remaining top plywood section. Squeeze a generous bead of wood glue along the frieze edge of the main shape; then place the rectangle of ¼-inch (6-mm)-plywood on the top. Press down firmly and check that all four edges line up correctly. Allow the glue to set a little, then secure the top with paneling nails at 2-inch (5-cm) intervals. Wipe away any excess glue.

11

Glue the two triangular roof supports to each end of the birdhouse top. Press the shapes down firmly onto the glue and wipe away any excess with a damp cloth. Once the glue has set a little, secure the support with a paneling nail hammered in at an angle at both points of the triangle shape.

12

Apply a generous bead of wood glue along the edges of each roof support and the angled apex edge of both roof sections. Place the two roof sections in position, so that the angled edges meet neatly at the apex. Allow the glue to set a little; then secure the roof to the support with paneling nails and let the glue dry. Drill a pilot hole through the roof and support, about 1 inch (2.5 cm) in from the outer edge. You will need to do this at a slight angle.

Countersink the drill holes and insert wood screws to secure the roof. Fill the drill holes with wood filler and sand smooth when dry. Apply a coat of primer, then a topcoat of brilliant white.

Sandcastle

This playful castle is sure to bring back happy memories of family beach vacations. Its sloping sides create a shape that is a little different from the standard "house." But it is still easy to construct and a good exercise in creative birdhouse-making for those new to the hobby. There's plenty of room inside for a pair of small birds and their new family—as a finishing touch, why not make a little flag from painted fabric just to show that there's someone at home?

You will need:

- basic tool kit (*see pages 8–11*)
- Sandcastle template (*see page 164*)
- plain paper for templates
- one sheet ¹/₂-in. (12-mm)-thick plywood—2 x 4 ft (61 x 122 cm)
- approx. 8-in. (20-cm) length of ¹/₄-in. (6-mm)-diameter dowel for flagpole and perch
- wood glue
- approx. fifty 1-in. (2.5-cm) paneling nails
- wood filler
- 40-oz. (1-l) can primer
- coarse-, medium-, and fine-grade sandpaper
- sand-effect or textured spray paint
- waterproof craft glue
- household and artist's paintbrushes
- two 1¹/₂-in. (38-mm) brass flush hinges, plus fixing screws
- one 1-in. (2.5-cm) brass hanging bracket, plus fixing screws

First Steps | Trace and enlarge the templates provided on page 164 to full size; then cut out the paper pattern pieces and transfer the outlines to a sheet of ½-inch (12-mm)-thick plywood—be sure to mark any drill-hole positions with pencil dots, and the top section position with dotted lines on the inside. Carefully cut out the pieces using a jigsaw. Do not cut the battlements yet. The small rectangular sections will be

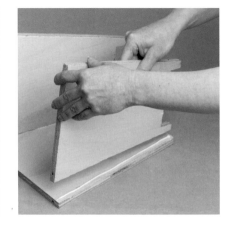

1

Use your jigsaw to cut diagonally across each space between the battlements as indicated by the lines on the template. This will leave a small triangle of plywood at the base of each space. Lay the sandcastle pieces on a safe surface, then place the blade of a narrow chisel on the horizontal line across the battlements. Strike the handle of the chisel with the side of your hammer to neatly chop away the waste.

2

Use a small strip of coarse-grade folded sandpaper to smooth away any rough edges on each battlement. Check that the edges are straight and that the battlements look even.

3

Lay the back section of the sandcastle on your work surface and apply a bead of wood glue next to each side edge. Place both side sections in place, then press down firmly onto the glue. Wipe away any excess glue with a damp cloth. While the glue is still wet, you can adjust the position of the sides so that the joint is straight.

removed with a chisel after the main pieces have been cut out. Use a medium-grade sandpaper to smooth any rough edges. Drill an access hole where indicated on the front section using the technique described for Basic Shape 1 (*see page 20*), and sand the cut edges smooth.

NOTE

It is a good idea to practice a few cuts with the chisel on a spare piece of plywood first before attempting to cut out the sandcastle shapes.

4

Once the glue has set, flip the shape over as shown above. Drive in a few paneling nails through the edge of the back section and down into the side sections to secure the joint at approximately 2-inch (5-cm) intervals. Wipe away any excess glue.

5

Turn the shape over again so it is lying on its back. Take the square top section and slot it in place using the dotted pencil lines as a guide for positioning. This piece should fit snugly, but if it is slightly large, sand the edges down to make a better fit. Remove the top section and apply a generous bead of glue to three sides, replacing it in position as before.

6

Turn the sandcastle shape on its side and secure one side of the top section using paneling nails driven in at approximately 2-inch (5-cm) intervals. Flip the shape over again and secure the other side of the top section. Finally, place the shape on its front and secure the back edge with paneling nails as before.

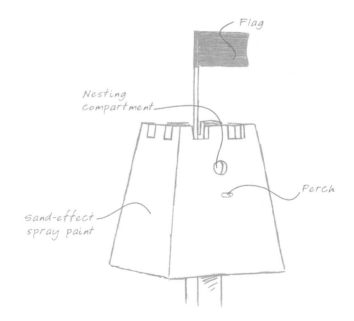

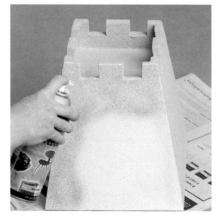

7

Turn the sandcastle over again so it is now lying on its back. Apply a generous bead of glue along both side edges, then place the front section in position. Press down firmly and allow the glue to set a little. Secure with a few paneling nails driven in at intervals along both sides as shown above.

8

The top/roof section must be watertight or the birds will have water leaking into their nest! Squeeze a generous bead of wood glue into the angle between the side walls and the top. Smooth this out with the tip of your finger to seal any gaps. Allow the glue to dry completely, forming a good watertight seal.

9

Fill all joints and voids with wood filler, then sand smooth when dry. Wipe away any dust particles with a damp cloth. Next prime and sand smooth using a fine-grade sandpaper. Apply a second coat of primer. Finally, apply a coat of sand-effect spray paint outdoors or in a well-ventilated room.

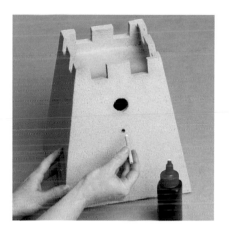

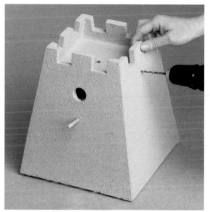

10

Using a small hacksaw, cut a 2-inch (5-cm) length of dowel for the perch. Sand both cut edges smooth. Apply a little wood glue to one end of the dowel and insert it into the predrilled perch hole just below the entrance hole on the sandcastle front. The fit should be quite snug so use a hammer to tap it into the hole if it is a little tight.

11

The sandcastle has a flat roof surrounded by shaped battlements at the top. This area will eventually collect rainwater, and while the birds might like to take a bath in it, the water may cause damage to the structure.

To remedy this, simply drill large drainage holes on both sides and at the back. Position the drill bit about halfway down the side/back as shown, and drill through to the other side. Any water should run safely through the holes.

12

Use a hacksaw to cut an 8-inch (20-cm)-long piece of dowel for the flagpole. Make a flag from a small piece of colorful fabric or paper and then paint it with waterproof craft glue to seal it. When dry, glue one end to the top of the pole. Apply a little wood glue to the lower edge of the pole and insert it into the predrilled hole in the center of the sandcastle top.

Pyramid

The fascinating pyramids of ancient Egypt have held their secrets for centuries. An enduring mystery is how the Egyptians managed to build these magnificent monuments. Building a pyramid on a smaller scale, however, presents less of a problem. Follow these simple instructions carefully to create a fabulous golden home for your feathered friends.

You will need:

- basic tool kit (*see pages 8–11*)
- Pyramid template (*see pages 164–165*)
- plain paper for templates
- one sheet $1/2$-in. (12-mm)-thick plywood—2 x 4 ft (61 x 122 cm)
- approx. 12-in. (30-cm) square of $1/4$-in. (6-mm)-thick plywood
- approx. 4-ft (122-cm) length of $5/8$ x $11/2$-in. (19 x 38-mm) strip lumber
- approx 6-in. (15-cm) length of $1/2$ x $1/2$-in. (12 x 12-mm)-square dowel for roof support
- wood glue
- approx. fifty 1-in. (2.5-cm) paneling nails
- wood filler
- 40-oz. (1-l) can primer
- medium- and fine-grade sandpaper
- one can metallic gold spray paint
- household paintbrush
- two $11/2$-in. (38-mm) brass flush hinges, plus fixing screws
- one 1-in. (2.5-cm) brass hanging bracket, plus fixing screws

First Steps | Trace and enlarge the templates provided on pages 164–165 to full size; then cut out the paper pattern pieces and transfer the outlines to a sheet of $^{1}/_{2}$-inch (12-mm)-thick plywood and $^{1}/_{4}$-inch (6-mm)-thick plywood as directed. Be sure to mark any drill-hole positions with pencil dots. Carefully cut out the pieces using a jigsaw. Use a medium-grade sandpaper to smooth any rough or splintered edges, especially along the

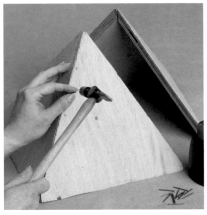

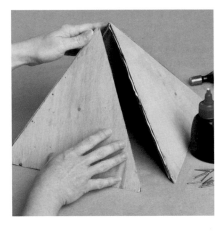

1

Gather the four triangular side sections. Apply a generous bead of wood glue to one side of one piece, then press another side section to it to form half the pyramid shape. You may need to hold the shape together for a few minutes while the glue begins to set or bind them with a few pieces of masking tape. Join the remaining two side sections in the same way.

Allow the glue to set completely, then drive in paneling nails at 2-inch (5-cm) intervals along the joint to hold the sections together.

2

Apply a bead of wood glue along the edge of one half of the pyramid shape then press the two halves together. Again, you may need to hold the shape together while the glue sets or use masking tape. The base of the pyramid shape should now be square.

3

When the glue has set, secure the shape with paneling nails hammered at 2-inch (5-cm) intervals. The triangular shapes can be difficult to align with each other, especially if your cutting lines are not completely straight. Any gaps will be remedied in the next stage. Set the shape aside and allow the glue to dry completely.

45-degree-angle cut. Using the jigsaw at an angle can be tricky and sometimes leave an untidy edge. Drill an access hole where indicated on the front section using the technique described for Basic Shape 1 (*see page 20*), and sand the cut edges smooth.

(*see page 20*)

NOTE

All of the edges of the four main triangular side sections are cut using the baseplate of the jigsaw set to an angle of approximately 45 degrees. This is to allow the edges to fit neatly together.

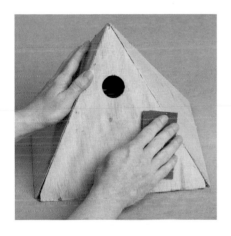

4

Apply generous amounts of wood filler to all four joints, using the flexible blade of the putty knife to press the product down into any small gaps or cracks. Check the surface of each side section to find any small holes or prominent wood grain. Fill all surface irregularities, then sand smooth when dry.

5

To make the lower plinth for the pyramid, join four strips of wood to form a rectangular frame. Cut two 12¾-inch (32.5-cm) and two 10-inch (25.5-cm) lengths and sand all cut edges smooth. Place the shorter strips so that they will form each end and position the longer strips in between, running along each side. Apply a little wood glue to the joints and allow to dry.

6

Apply a generous bead of wood glue close to the inner edge of the plinth. Place the rectangular base section with the cutout center area on top of the plinth, pressing firmly down onto the bead of glue. The base has one slightly wider edge, which should be at the front.

While the glue is still wet, position the base section so that there is an equal amount of the plinth allowed all around, forming a neat step. Secure the base to the plinth with paneling nails.

Entry to nesting compartment

Palm trees

Platform

Metallic gold spray paint

7

Apply a bead of glue around the inner edge of the base section. Place the pyramid shape onto the glue and press it down firmly. Wipe away any excess glue with a damp cloth. When the glue has set a little, use a few paneling nails to hold the shape to the base.

Drill two pilot holes through the lower edge of the pyramid into the base at each side, countersink the holes, then drive a screw into each one to secure the shape to the base. Fill the holes with wood filler, then sand smooth when dry.

8

Cut out the palm-tree templates and trace the outlines onto a small sheet of ¼-inch (6-mm)-thick plywood. Use a jigsaw fitted with a blade suitable for tight curves to cut out the shapes. Remember, you'll need two trees—one a mirror image of the other. Cutting small shapes can be tricky, but if you work slowly and carefully you will get good results. Sand all cut edges smooth.

9

Using a small hacksaw, cut two 4-inch (10-cm) lengths of ½-inch (12-mm)-square dowel to act as supports for both the entrance roof and the palm trees that flank the entrance. Sand the cut edges smooth; then glue the pieces to the underside of the rectangular roof section as shown above.

10

Glue the roof and supports in position at the front of the pyramid. Nail the top of both supports to the roof from the top as shown. Hammer a few paneling nails in at an angle to secure the back of the roof to the side of the pyramid. Turn the shape upside down and drill a hole from the underside upward into the bottom of each roof support. Drive a long wood screw into each hole to secure the supports.

HINTS AND SUGGESTIONS

Although metallic gold spray paint works well for this elegant pyramid shape, you could opt for a textured sandstone paint for a more realistic effect. The palm trees could also be painted in realistic browns and greens if you are feeling creative!

11

Apply the first coat of primer, sand it smooth using a fine-grade sandpaper, then apply a second coat. A very smooth finish is required as a base for the metallic gold topcoat. Glue and nail the palm trees in position, then apply a coat of primer.

ATTRACTING INSECTS

Birds such as martins, flycatchers, swallows, and swifts feed and catch their food "on the wing," so be sure to include plants in your garden that will be attractive to insects, such as plaintain lilies.

12

Place the pyramid on a sheet of newspaper and apply a thin coat of gold metallic spray paint. Allow the first coat to dry before applying the next. Examine the finish at this stage and apply a third coat, if necessary. The shiny paint will accentuate any surface irregularities, so you may need to smooth out a few bumps using a fine-grade sandpaper after the first coat.

Space Rocket

Birds don't usually need much help getting airborne, but hopefully a tiny family will take a liking to this space rocket and make it home for a season or two. As an alternative to creating a space-age accommodation, you could cut a larger access hole and use the rocket as a feeder instead—simply fill with scraps, seeds, or a large fat ball. The basic shape of the rocket is made from empty plastic bottles—yet another opportunity for recycling.

You will need:

- basic tool kit (*see pages 8–11*)
- Space Rocket template (*see page 165*)
- plain paper for templates
- 6-in. (15-cm) square of ½-in. (12-mm)-thick plywood
- empty plastic water bottle (tall, slim shape)
- large plastic soda bottle (large, fat shape)
- approx. 8-in. (20-cm) length of 1-in. (2.5-cm)-diameter dowel for inner support
- wood glue
- waterproof marker
- 40-oz. (1-l) can primer
- medium-grade sandpaper
- one No. 6 1-in. (3.5 mm x 2.5-cm) wood screw

- sixteen No. 6 ½-in. (3.5 x 12-mm) domed brass wood screws
- six No. 2 ³/₈-in. (1.5 x 9.5-mm) countersunk brass wood screws
- ³/₄-in. (2-cm)-wide masking tape
- one can each of red and white enamel spray paint
- household paintbrush
- one large screw eye

First Steps | Trace and enlarge the templates provided on page 165 to full size; then cut out the paper pattern pieces and transfer the leg outlines to a sheet of ¹⁄₂-inch (12-mm)-thick plywood. Carefully cut out the pieces using a jigsaw. Use a medium-grade sandpaper to smooth any rough or splintered edges on the plywood leg sections, and cut off the bottle neck.

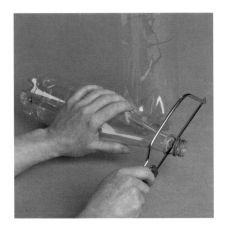

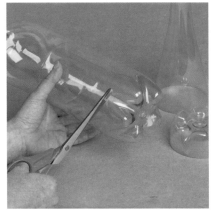

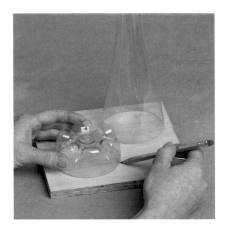

1

Remove any labels or glue residue from the plastic bottles and make sure that they are clean and dry inside. Use a small hacksaw to remove the thread at the top of the slim bottle. Smooth any rough edges using a medium-grade sandpaper.

2

Cut away the center section of the slim bottle and discard, keeping the neck and base as shown above. Cut off the top and base of the fatter bottle and keep the side section for the next stage. Cut the center section open so it forms a wide rectangular band.

3

Stand the neck and base of the slim bottle on a small square of ¹⁄₂-inch (12-mm)-thick plywood. Using a pencil, trace around the outside to create two circular shapes. Remember to indicate on each shape if it is the top or the bottom because they may be slightly different sizes. Carefully cut out the two circles using a jigsaw. Sand the cut edges smooth using a medium-grade sandpaper.

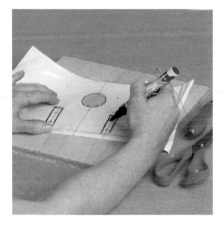

4

Place the bottom circle inside the plastic base as shown. Cut a length of dowel to fit inside the neck, reaching from the lower edge to the hole at the top. Drill a pilot hole through the center of the remaining circle and one into the center of the dowel.

Apply wood glue to the drilled end of the dowel support, then position it in the center of the circle. Screw the support in place as shown above.

5

Apply a generous amount of glue to the top end of the dowel support and place it inside the neck of the bottle. The glue will seal the hole at the top of the neck to prevent any water from trickling down inside the body of the rocket.

6

Place the rectangular side band from the fatter bottle on top of the template with the entrance hole and leg positions. Using a waterproof marker, trace the outline of the entrance hole onto the plastic and indicate the leg and screw hole positions. Remove the template and cut out the circular entrance hole using scissors; then use the awl to pierce pilot holes through the plastic where indicated.

7

Screw each leg to the plastic side band using two small brass screws. This is a little tricky because the band is curved and springy. It is a good idea to secure one leg at a time with a small piece of double-sided adhesive tape. This will hold it temporarily while you drill a small pilot hole at each screw position to prepare for the screws to follow.

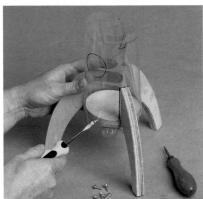

8

Wrap the side band around the base section and pierce a pilot hole at the center front—between the legs and into the plywood circle. Drill a small hole, then insert a brass roundheaded screw to hold the side section in place. Neatly overlap the ends of the side section at the back and insert a screw through both layers into the plywood circle. Insert screws at regularly spaced intervals to hold the base in place.

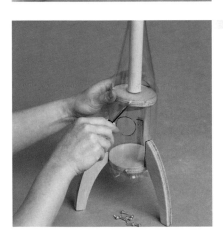

9

Ease the top part of the rocket inside the side band as shown. Insert fixing screws through both layers of plastic and into the plywood circle. Use the position of the screws that hold the base in place as a positioning guide.

HINTS AND SUGGESTIONS

When fall arrives, simply loosen the screws that hold the base to the body of the rocket to clean the interior.

You can also use this method to insert a large fat ball—if you intend to use the rocket as a feeder. The birds can peck at the food but cannot make off with the whole thing in one shot! See page 107 for the recipe.

10

Mark the center of the dowel support at the neck of the bottle with a pencil dot. Drill a pilot hole into the center of the dowel to match the diameter of the thread of the large hanging eye. Insert the tip of the eye into the hole and screw it into the dowel. Because the rocket is lightweight, the screw will not pull free.

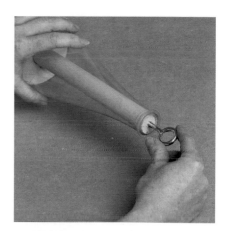

11

Make sure that the plastic surfaces are dry, clean, and free of grease marks or dust particles because the spray paint layer will accentuate all surface irregularities. Apply a coat of white spray primer, and allow it to dry completely. Next apply a coat of gloss white spray paint and allow it to dry completely.

12

Wrap strips of masking tape in equally spaced horizontal bands around the main body of the rocket. Cut smaller pieces to fit between each leg. Stand the rocket up and apply one thin coat of gloss red spray paint. Allow this coat to dry before applying a second coat, if necessary. Carefully peel the tape away when the paint is completely dry.

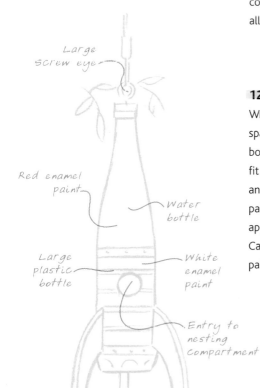

Large Screw eye

Red enamel paint

Water bottle

Large plastic bottle

White enamel paint

Entry to nesting compartment

Tea Party Feeder

Invite your feathered friends to a tea party in the backyard! This bird feeder is very easy to construct—the secret lies in having a steady hand to paint the checkered pattern on the tablecloth. However, if checks and stripes are not to your taste, make up a freestyle floral pattern of your own or try polka dots instead. Use a child's plastic tea set to hold water and seeds for the birds' feast.

You will need:

- basic tool kit (*see pages 8–11*)
- Tea Party Feeder template (*see page 165*)
- plain paper for templates
- one sheet 1/2-in. (12-mm)-thick plywood—2 x 4 ft (61 x 122 cm)
- approx. thirty 1-in. (2.5-cm) paneling nails
- wood glue
- wood filler
- 40-oz. (1-l) can primer
- medium- and fine-grade sandpaper
- 40-oz. (1-l) cans yellow and red latex-based exterior-grade paint
- household and artist's paintbrushes
- child's plastic tea set

First Steps | Trace and enlarge the templates provided on page 165 to full size; then cut out the paper pattern pieces and transfer the outlines to a sheet of ½-inch (12-mm)-thick plywood. Carefully cut out the pieces using a jigsaw. Use a medium-grade sandpaper to smooth any rough or splintered edges. Fill all the voids that you may see along the cut edges with wood filler, then sand smooth when dry. Wipe

1

When the first coat is dry, you can sand it smooth using a fine-grade sandpaper, then apply a second coat of primer. Apply two coats of the yellow base color over the primer, allowing the first to dry before applying the second. Turn each side piece over and apply yellow paint to the reverse side in the same way.

2

Using a ruler and pencil, draw the first set of parallel stripes that will form the check pattern on the tablecloth. Make the stripes about ½ inch (12 mm) wide and space them approximately 1 inch (2.5 cm) apart. Begin at the center of the tabletop section and work outward in both directions so the stripe pattern will be symmetrical.

3

Next, use the ruler and pencil to draw a set of parallel stripes on the tabletop section to cross the first set at right angles. Use the same measurements and spacing so the check pattern will be even and regular across the entire section.

away any dust particles with a damp cloth before applying the first coat of primer to one side of the tabletop and both sides of each side section. Any dust particles that are left on the surface will ultimately spoil the smooth surface finish.

> **NOTE**
>
> *It is very important to check that all voids are filled properly because they may allow moisture to penetrate the plywood sections, which in time will cause the layers to separate and damage all of your hard work.*

4

Draw horizontal stripes on each of the four side sections. Take care not to take the lines all the way to the outside edges, since the design shows a fold in the tablecloth here. These lines need to be drawn freehand. For the vertical stripes, match the sides to the tabletop section.

5

Using the photograph on page 97 as a guide, draw the curved stripes at each corner to resemble a fold in the "fabric" of the tablecloth. Do not take the stripes around the edge of the side pieces yet—this will be easier to do when the table is fully constructed.

6

Begin painting in the red stripes. Take your time as you do this, working from one side of the tabletop section across to the other, closely following the pencil lines with your paintbrush. Don't worry if your lines are a little wobbly—they won't show too much when the other set of stripes is completed.

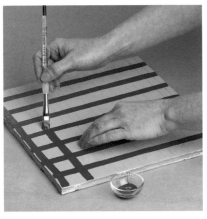   

7

Allow the first painted stripes to dry completely, then apply the second set—crossing the first at right angles. If your measurements are accurate, the red stripes should form a neat check pattern with even yellow squares. Set the tabletop aside to allow the paint to dry.

8

Apply red paint to all the vertical and horizontal stripes on the four sides, leaving the end sections unpainted at this stage. Use a more flowing paint stroke to fill in the "folds" at each end when the main part is completed. When the paint is dry, flip the pieces over and continue the stripes along the top edge and approximately 1 inch (2.5 cm) down the reverse side.

9

Apply wood glue to the edge of the tabletop along two opposite sides. Place one side section facedown on your work surface. Place the tabletop onto the side section, pressing the glued edge to it about ½ inch (12 mm) from the straight top edge, matching up the stripe pattern carefully. This will form a small lip around the tabletop. Position the other side section in the same way.

Allow the glue to dry, then nail the sides sections to the tabletop. Glue and nail the remaining two sides to the tabletop in the same way.

Plastic tea pot

Plastic cups to hold water

Plastic saucer to hold bird feed

Yellow paint

Red paint

10

Use your artist's paintbrush and the red paint to fill in the narrow strip that runs along the edge of each side section at the corners. Use flowing brushstokes to make sure that the stripes match up, and the corner fold looks correct.

11

The shallow lip that surrounds the tabletop prevents seeds and other food from falling off the table. However, it will also collect rainwater, which will eventually cause damage to the surface. Drill large drainage holes as shown above, through the tabletop to allow any rainwater to drain away safely.

12

Finally, set the table for your tea party! Use a generous amount of glue to secure a teapot, teacups, saucers, and perhaps a small plate, to the tabletop. You can also cut a large hole in the side of the teapot for small birds.

Swimming Pool Feeder

Your feathered friends may like to take a bath before or after dinner—and it's so much fun to watch them splashing in the water! Birds love bathing, and they love fresh fruit, too, and this is an amusing and unusual way to provide them with both. The inspiration for this project is a 1950s outdoor swimming pool. Our pool has a simple apple feeder along the back edge that is designed to resemble a row of little changing rooms.

You will need:

- basic tool kit (*see pages 8–11*)
- Swimming Pool Feeder template (*see page 166*)
- plain paper for templates
- one sheet 1/2-in. (12-mm)-thick plywood—2 x 4 ft (61 x 122cm)
- approx. 6 x 18-in. (15 x 45.5-cm) length of 1/4-in. (6-mm)-thick plywood
- 3/4 x 1/2-in. (18 x 12-mm) wooden strips for apple feeder supports or cut from the 1/2-in. (12-mm)-thick plywood
- wood glue
- appprox. eighty 1-in. (2.5-cm) paneling nails
- approx. ten 1-in. (2.5-cm) fine finishing nails
- eight No. 6 1-in. (3.5 mm x 2.5-cm) wood screws
- wood filler

- 40-oz. (1-l) can primer
- medium-grade sandpaper
- waterproof grout and tile adhesive
- grout spreader
- approx. six hundred 3/4-in. (2-cm) square yellow, blue, and green mosaic tiles
- 40-oz. (1-l) cans green and yellow latex-based exterior-grade paint
- one long metal skewer
- household and artist's paintbrushes

First Steps | Trace and enlarge the templates provided on page 166 to full size; then cut out the paper pattern pieces and transfer the outlines to a sheet of ½-inch (12-mm)-thick and ¼-inch (6-mm)-thick plywood as directed. Indicate the inner pool positioning lines on the base using dotted pencil lines. Carefully cut out the pieces using a jigsaw; then cut out the central section of the pool top using a spade

1

Glue and nail together the four pool side sections to make a rectangular frame as shown above. Apply a generous bead of glue close to the edge of the cutout section in the center of the pool top. Place the frame in position and press it down firmly onto the glue. While the glue is wet, adjust the frame so the inner edges are flush with the cut edge of the top. Allow the glue to dry.

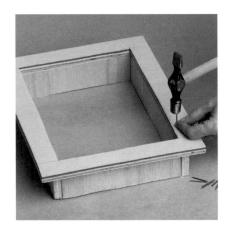

2

When the glue has set a little, flip the shape over and insert paneling nails at approximately 1-inch (2.5-cm) intervals in order to secure the pool top to the inner sides of the pool. Wipe away any excess glue using a damp cloth.

3

Turn the shape upside down in order to secure the pool base in position. Apply a generous bead of glue along the edge of the inner pool sides; then press the base in position, making sure that the sides of the pool correspond with the dotted positioning lines (refer to the template on page 166) on the pool base. Nail the base in position using paneling nails at approximately 2-inch (5-cm) intervals.

bit to drill a hole in each corner through which the jigsaw can be inserted. Use a medium-grade sandpaper to smooth any rough or splintered edges, and use a damp cloth to wipe away the dust particles.

4

Take the side, back, and front sections to complete the basic shape. Glue the shorter side sections to the shape as shown above, then nail securely in place. Be sure to use plenty of wood glue because this will serve to seal the joint in addition to holding the whole shape together.

5

Glue and nail the two remaining pieces to the front and back of the pool as shown. Wipe away any excess glue with a damp cloth, then allow for the glue to set completely. When dry, turn the pool over so it is right-side up again.

6

Fill all joints and voids along the exposed cut edges with wood filler, using the flexible blade to press the product down into any gaps or cracks. Use medium-grade sandpaper to sand all surfaces smooth when the filler is dry. Wipe away any dust particles with a damp cloth. It is not necessary to prime this shape.

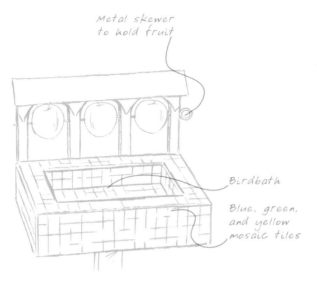

Metal skewer
to hold fruit

Birdbath

Blue, green,
and yellow
mosaic tiles

HINTS AND SUGGESTIONS

• *As an alternative to apples, you could thread three small fat balls (see right for recipe) onto the skewer that passes though the arched feeder at the back of the swimming pool. While fruit is perfectly acceptable, high-energy fat is valuable to birds during the winter months when other food sources may be scarce.*

• *Be very sure that the grout between the tiles is sound. Any gaps may allow water to penetrate to the plywood beneath.*

7

Apply the mosaic tiles to the basic pool shape in a simple geometric design. Use the photograph on page 103 as a guide, or try making up your own design. Apply a little adhesive to the back of each tile, then press it into position. Cover the front and top of the pool, then glue the tiles to the inner walls. Leave the back untiled for the moment.

8

Cut four 11-inch (25.5-cm) lengths of wood for the apple-feeder supports. Use the miter saw to cut one end of each to an angle of 45 degrees. Sand all the cut edges smooth; then drill a hole through each strip 7 inches (18 cm) away from the straight cut end. This will provide a channel for the metal skewer that holds the apples in position.

Drill and countersink two screw holes in the back of each strip about 1 inch (2.5 cm) and 2 inches (5 cm) from the straight cut end as shown above.

9

Apply a coat of primer to the shaped feeder section, the supports, and the roof. When the primer is dry, apply two coats of green paint to the four supports and curved section. Apply yellow paint to the roof. Set the pieces to one side and allow all the paint to dry.

Suet/fat balls

High-energy foods are essential to wild birds during the colder months when natural food is scarce and inclement weather conditions may make it difficult for small birds to search for sustenance.

Ingredients

2 cups of suet or or any hard fat

1½ cups of seed mix

(start off with this ratio, then increase according to need)

Melt the suet or fat in a small saucepan and stir in the seed mix to form a stiff consistency. Spoon the mixture into a mold, such as an ice-cube tray, a small can, or a plastic pot, or just allow it to cool and mold it into a ball with your hands. Larger molds can be placed directly on the feeder, while balls and small cubes can be removed from the mold and threaded on string.

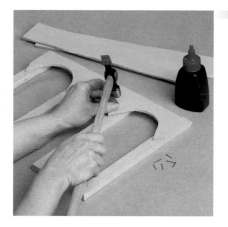

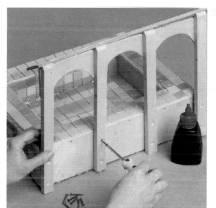

10

Arrange the supports with the angled end at the top. Glue the shaped feeder section to the supports as shown, then secure each in place using veneer nails. Apply a small amount of glue to the angled section at the top of each support and place the roof section in position. Drive a paneling nail through the roof down into the support beneath to secure it in place. Set aside to allow the glue to dry.

11

Turn the pool so the back is facing you, then position the feeder as shown. Use the awl to pierce a pilot hole in the pool side using the predrilled and countersunk holes as a guide. Screw the feeder securely in place using the wood screws. Fill in the spaces between the supports with mosaic tiles as before.

12

Apply grout to the small gaps between each mosaic tile, using a spreader with a flexible rubber blade. Take up a small amount of grout on the blade and press it onto the tiles; the grout will be squeezed into the spaces, providing a good waterproof seal. Wipe away excess grout with a damp cloth or sponge. Make sure to fill all the gaps well so water will not seep or leak out.

Tower Feeder

This shiny, futuristic feeder is reminiscent of tall observation towers seen in many large cities. The shape is basically built from disks of plywood supported with dowels and clad with a shaped band of sleek aluminum. This design is suitable for mounting on a tall pole in your backyard or perhaps closer to your home on a patio or on a balcony. Birds will be attracted to the shiny metal finish and then be pleased to find the goodies ready for them to eat inside.

You will need:

- basic tool kit (*see pages 8–11*)
- Tower Feeder template (*see page 167*)
- plain paper for templates
- half sheet ½-in. (12-mm)-thick plywood—2 x 2 ft (61 x 61 cm)
- 4-in. (10-cm) length of ⅜-in. (9-mm)-diameter dowel for top spike
- wood glue
- approx. twenty 1-in. (2.5-cm) paneling nails
- wood filler
- 40-oz. (1-l) can primer
- medium- and fine-grade sandpaper
- one can silver spray paint
- household and artist's paintbrushes
- sheet thin aluminum
- tin snips
- sixteen No. 6 ½-in. (3.5 x 12-mm)-long chrome slotted roundhead wood screws
- eight No. 6 1½-in. (3.5 x 40-mm)-long wood screws

First Steps | Trace and enlarge the templates provided on page 167 to full size.

Be sure to mark the dowel-support positions and the base position. Cut out the paper pattern pieces and transfer the outlines to a sheet of ½-inch (12-mm)-thick plywood. Carefully cut out the pieces using a jigsaw. Use a medium-grade sandpaper to smooth any rough or splintered edges.

1

Take the ring-shaped base and apply a generous bead of glue close to the inner cutout edge. Place the smaller circular disk that will form the base on top of the ring, making sure that there is an equal margin all the way around. Press the base firmly onto the ring, then wipe away any excess glue with a damp cloth. Turn the shape over and nail the ring securely to the base as shown above.

2

Cut a 5-inch (13-cm) length of dowel; then sand both cut edges smooth. Drill a large hole—to match the diameter of the dowel—in the center of the smallest disk. Apply a little wood glue to one end of the dowel and insert it into the predrilled hole. Use a hammer to tap the dowel into the hole because it may be a tight fit.

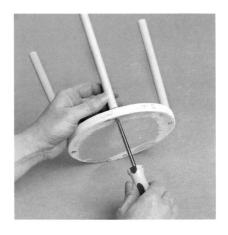

3

Now cut four 7-inch (18-cm) lengths of dowel for the central feeder supports, and sand both cut ends smooth. Glue one end of each support in position on the central feeder base as shown above (refer to the template on page 167 for positioning). Next drill a pilot hole up through the base and into each of the dowels. Insert a wood screw into each of the pilot holes to secure the dowels in place.

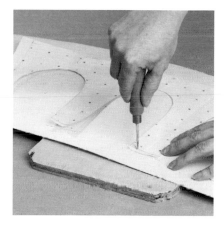

4

Place the central feeder top in position and drill pilot holes downward through the top and into each dowel. Insert a wood screw into each of the screw holes as shown above to complete the basic structure of the central feeder. Make sure that all the screws are tight and secure.

5

Fill any voids along the cut edges with wood filler, then sand smooth when the filler is dry. Wipe away any dust particles with a damp cloth before applying two coats of primer, sanding in between coats with a fine-grade sandpaper. Apply one or two thin coats of metallic spray paint, allowing the first coat to dry before applying the second.

6

Attach the feeder side template to a sheet of thin aluminum using small pieces of masking tape. Leave the protective film on the metal at this stage. Trace around the edge of the template. Next use your awl to make pilot holes through the metal where indicated. Make sure that the metal is placed on a scrap of plywood while you do this to protect your work surface.

7

Use a tin snip to cut the metal shape carefully along the traced outline. The metal is soft and malleable and is not difficult to cut or shape. Cut the top and lower edge first, then tackle the curved arch shapes. Make each cut smooth and accurate because the ragged edges may be sharp.

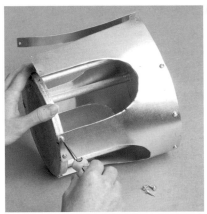

8

Wrap the metal shape around the central feeder, overlapping the edges at the back as shown. Use the point of the awl to pierce pilot holes in the edge of the plywood disk beneath, using each previously pierced hole as a guide. Insert a small roundhead screw into each hole to secure the metal to the central feeder shape.

9

Turn the central feeder shape upside down and apply wood glue to the underside. Place the base section from step 1 in place on the feeder, then press down firmly. Secure the base to the feeder with a few paneling nails as shown. You can use screws instead if you prefer—simply drill a small pilot hole first and then drive in the screw securely.

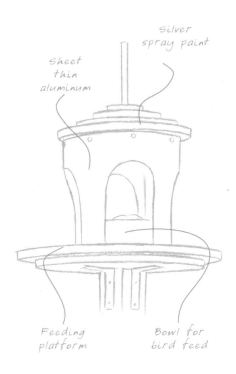

Silver spray paint

Sheet thin aluminum

Feeding platform

Bowl for bird feed

KEEP FEEDING!

If you begin feeding wild birds, be sure to keep up the effort. They will quickly become dependent on the food source and will suffer if the supply is suddenly withdrawn.

10

Once the glue has set, turn the shape over so it stands the right side up. Apply wood glue to the center of the feeder top; then place the largest of the remaining disks onto the glue. Press down firmly and wipe away any excess glue using a damp cloth. Allow the glue to set a little; then hold the shape in place using a few paneling nails.

11

Secure the remaining disks, in size order, to the top of the feeder to make a neat, stepped shape. Glue and nail each layer securely, wiping away excess glue with a damp cloth. Any glue spots will dry hard and white, spoiling the metallic-paint finish.

FEEDING GARLAND

You can make a pretty garland of tasty treats for the birds by threading pieces of fruit such as apples, oranges, peaches, cranberries, plums, or grapes together with popped popcorn, cooked potatoes, small bread balls, or fat balls (see page 107) onto a strong length of garden twine. Hang the garland from a tree branch in a position where you can watch the birds while they feed.

12

Glue the smallest disk with the dowel spire to the top of the feeder. Allow the glue to dry before securing the shape in place with two paneling nails.

Mediterranean Feeder

This classical form evokes glorious summer vacations spent along the Mediterranean Sea. The pristine white walls and archways of this sturdy feeder are topped with glossy blue domes typical of this style of architecture. Elegant yet functional, this easy-to-construct feeder provides a perfect receptacle for lots of tasty goodies for hungry garden visitors.

You will need:

- basic tool kit (*see pages 8–11*)
- Mediterranean Feeder template (*see page 168*)
- plain paper for templates
- one sheet 1/2-in. (12-mm)-thick plywood—2 x 2 ft (61 x 61 cm)
- half sheet 1/4-in. (6-mm)-thick plywood—2 x 4 ft (61 x 122 cm)
- 1-yd. (91.5-cm) length of 1 x 3-in. (2.5 x 7.5-cm) lumber for corners
- 1-yd. (91.5-cm) length of 1 x 2-in. (2.5 x 5-cm) lumber for corners
- approx. 10-in. (25.5-cm) length of 1-in. (2.5-cm)-diameter dowel for dome support
- old plastic ball approx. 7 in. (18 cm) in diameter
- four round plastic laundry-detergent balls or small plastic playground balls
- wood glue

- approx. forty 1-in. (2.5-cm) paneling nails
- approx. four 1-in. (2.5-cm) finishing nails
- wood filler
- 40-oz. (1-l) can primer
- medium- and fine-grade sandpaper
- 40-oz. (1-l) can latex-based exterior-grade white paint
- one can blue spray paint
- household paintbrushes
- stapler

First Steps | Trace and enlarge the templates provided on page 168 to full size; then cut out the paper pattern pieces and transfer the outlines to a sheet of ¹/₂-inch (12-mm)-thick plywood and ¹/₄-inch (6-mm)-thick plywood as directed. Be sure to mark any drill-hole positions with pencil dots. Carefully cut out the pieces using a jigsaw. Use a medium-grade sandpaper to smooth any rough or splintered edges.

1

Using scissors, cut the large ball in half; discard the half that contains the air valve. Trim each of the laundry detergent balls to form a neat half-dome shape. Make sure that all of the surfaces are clean, dry, and free of dirt and grease.

2

Apply a coat of primer to the large ball and allow it to dry. Place the large ball and the smaller plastic domes on a sheet of newspaper and apply a thin coat of blue spray paint. Examine the finish when the paint is dry and, if necessary, apply a second coat. Always use spray paint in a well-ventilated area.

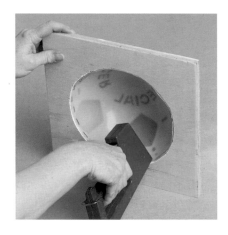

3

Apply a generous bead of glue around the circular cut edge in the center of the top section of the building. Slip the large ball inside the cutout area and press the edge onto the glue bead. Fix the ball in place using a stapler as shown—alternatively, you can use paneling nails.

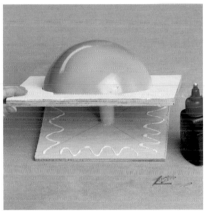

4

Next, take the ¼-inch (6-mm)-thick plywood square that forms the dome support and glue a length of dowel, measuring about half the diameter of the ball, to the center. Drill a pilot hole up through the underside of the square into the dowel. Insert a screw into the hole to hold the dowel secure.

5

Apply a generous bead of glue to the underside of the temple top section and place it over the dome support. Secure the support to the top with paneling nails. The dowel will prevent the dome shape from collapsing.

6

Glue and nail the sides of the temple to the front and back section as shown. The resulting structure should be square, each side measuring 10 inches (25.5 cm). Use a damp cloth to wipe away any glue that may have seeped out.

PINECONE FEEDER

This is so simple to make, yet it is very effective. Find a large pinecone and shake it to remove any loose seeds or organic debris. Tie a length of garden twine around the cone and make a hanging loop at the end. Spread peanut butter all over the cone, pressing it down between the scales. Roll the cone in a seed mix to complete. Most birds will love this feeder and will pick it clean in record time. Refill when empty.

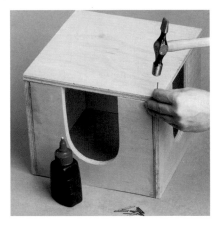

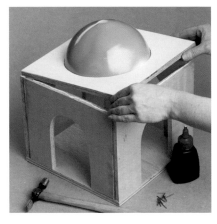

7

Turn the arched shape upside down and apply a bead of glue to the lower edges. Place the base section in position and secure by driving in paneling nails at approximately 2-inch (5-cm) intervals around the edge. When the glue has dried, sand the edge of the base section so it lies completely flush with the side walls.

8

Turn the shape the right side up, and glue and nail the domed top section in place in the same way. Again, when the glue is dry, sand the edge so it lies flush with the side walls. Fill all joints and voids with wood filler and sand them smooth when dry. Wipe away any dust particles with a damp cloth before applying two coats of primer, sanding the shape smooth using a fine-grade sandpaper.

9

Take the 1 x 3-inch and 1 x 2-inch lengths of wood and cut four 9-inch (23-cm) lengths from each to form the corner pillars. Sand all the cut edges smooth with a medium-grade sandpaper.

Apply a generous amount of wood glue to one side of the four 1 x 2-inch pieces and position them on both sides of the arch on the front and the back of the shape. Attach the 1 x 3-inch pieces in place in the same way to the remaining two sides to complete the corner pillars. When the glue is dry, drive in a few paneling nails to hold each piece in place.

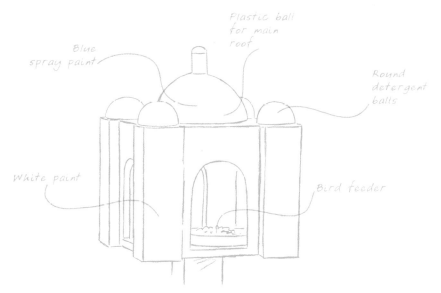

Blue spray paint

Plastic ball for main roof

Round detergent balls

White paint

Bird feeder

10

Fill all joints and voids with wood filler, then sand smooth when dry. Wipe away any dust particles using a damp cloth before applying two coats of primer, sanding in between coats. When the primer is dry, apply topcoats of white paint, allowing each coat to dry before applying the next.

11

Cut four short lengths of dowel—each measuring the height of the small domes. Glue one of the dowel supports close to each corner of the feeder shape. Apply a small amount of glue to the top of each support, then position a small dome onto each one. Allow the glue to dry; then secure each of the domes to its support using a fine finishing nail.

12

Cut a 2 inch (5-cm) length of dowel and sand one end to a smooth, round shape with medium-grade sandpaper. Paint the dowel white, and when the paint is dry, add blue paint to the shaped top. Glue the small tower to the center of the large dome to complete the temple feeder.

High-Rise Feeder

A modernist skyscraper with feeding stations at varying levels all the way up provides easy access to food for many birds at a time. Mirrored tiles have been added to create surface interest and to produce the effect of the many windows in a multistory building. This feeder would be an elegant addition to the patio or balcony of a sleek, modern home. The streetwise city slickers of the feathered variety will love it!

You will need:

- basic tool kit (*see pages 8–11*)
- High-Rise Feeder template (*see page 168*)
- plain paper for templates
- one sheet ½-in. (12-mm)-thick plywood—2 x 4 ft (61 x 122 cm)
- 12-in. (30-cm) length of 2 x 2-in. (51 x 51-mm) lumber for stepped top
- 6-in. (15-cm) length of ³⁄₈-in. (9-mm)-diameter dowel for the top spire
- wood glue
- approx. forty 1-in. (2.5-cm) paneling nails
- wood filler
- 40-oz. (1-l) can primer
- medium- and fine-grade sandpaper
- one can of stone-effect spray paint
- household paintbrush
- approx. one hundred and seventy ½-in. (12-mm)-square mirror mosaic tiles

First Steps | Trace and enlarge the templates provided on page 168 to full size; then cut out the paper pattern pieces. Make sure that you copy all of the dotted lines that indicate the floor positions onto the template. Transfer the outlines to a sheet of ¹/₂-inch (12-mm)-thick plywood. Carefully cut out the pieces with a jigsaw, using the method described on page 14 to cut out the windows. It is useful at this stage to mark the dotted

1

Cut three 3¹/₂-inch (9-cm) lengths from the square lumber, and one 5-inch (12.5-cm) length of dowel. The rectangular blocks will form the stepped tower shape at the top of the feeder. Use medium-grade sandpaper to smooth all cut edges, including the edges around the windows.

2

Take the back, the side sections without the cutout windows, and the double window side. Glue them together as shown above, then secure the shapes using paneling nails at approximately 2-inch (5-cm) intervals.

3

Slot both floors into position using the dotted lines as a guide. The pieces should fit snugly, but if they are a little large it is simple to sand the sides down to create a better fit. Apply glue to the edges of the floor sections, then position each one carefully.

Allow the glue to dry, then nail the floors in place. You may choose to mark the floor position on the outside walls as a guide to ensure that the nail does not miss its target.

lines that indicate the floor positions on both sides of the cutout side sections. This acts as a guide when you are nailing the floor sections in place. Use a medium-grade sandpaper to smooth any rough or splintered edges, then wipe away all of the dust particles with a damp cloth. Take care to keep the sandpaper flat in your hand while you do this so that you don't round off any of the cut edges—this design is intended to look sharp and sleek.

4

Apply a generous bead of wood glue to both long edges of the remaining wall section and slot it in place as shown above. Nail it securely. Wipe away any glue that may have seeped out with a damp cloth. When the glue has dried, turn the shape upside down.

5

Apply a generous bead of glue to the lower edge of the feeder, and press the smaller base section into position as shown. The design allows an equal margin of ½ inch (12 mm) all around. While the glue is still wet, adjust the position of the square so the margin is equal. Nail the base in place as shown.

6

Apply a generous amount of glue to the center of the first base section and glue the remaining, slightly larger, base section in place. Again, a margin of ½ inch (12 mm) is allowed all around so be sure to make positioning adjustments while the glue is still wet. Use a few paneling nails to hold the base secure. Turn the shape right-side up.

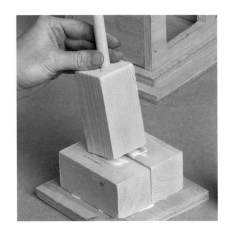

7

Use a pencil and ruler to draw diagonal lines from corner to corner across the top of one of the rectangular 4-inch (10-cm)-lumber blocks to find the center, then drill a large hole. The diameter of this hole should match the diameter of the dowel spire. Apply glue to the end of the dowel and insert it into the hole. Use a hammer to drive it in, if necessary. Wipe away any excess glue, then set it aside to dry.

8

While the spire is drying in the top block, apply glue to the center of the square top section and position the remaining two lumber sections side by side as shown above. When the glue is dry, turn the top upside down and drive in a few paneling nails from underneath to hold the blocks in place.

9

Place the top section the right side up and glue the top block, complete with spire, to the center as shown. When the glue has dried, drive a nail at an angle through the center of each side into the top to hold it secure.

HIGH-RISE FEEDING

*The High-Rise Feeder has three levels,
which offer three opportunities for
birds to gain access to food. If you
are new to bird feeding, you can
try different types of food or
mixes on each level.*

*Check every few days to see which
feed your garden visitors prefer—
you'll easily be able to tell this by
noting which seeds or food are
left behind and which have been
devoured without a trace. Fill up
with the favorites to encourage
the birds to return.*

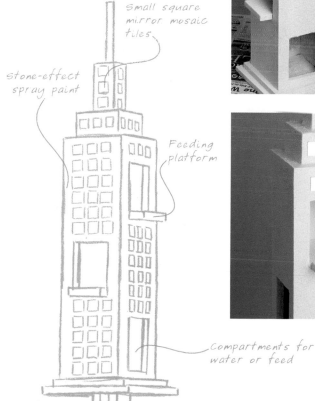

Small square
mirror mosaic
tiles

Stone-effect
spray paint

Feeding
platform

Compartments for
water or feed

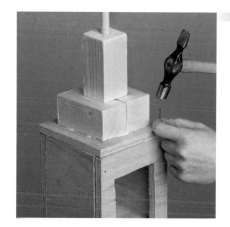

10

Apply a generous bead of glue to the top
edge of the feeder shape, and place the
stepped top section into position. Press
down firmly; then wipe away any glue
that may seep out with a damp cloth.
Allow the glue to dry a little before
nailing the top into place around the
edge as shown.

11

Fill all joints and voids with wood filler,
then sand smooth when dry. Wipe away
any dust particles with a damp cloth
before applying two coats of primer.
Sand the shape smooth using a fine-grade
sandpaper between coats. Apply a coat of
textured stone-effect spray paint. Always
use spray paint in a well-ventilated area.

12

When the textured-paint finish has dried,
glue the small, square mirror mosaic tiles in
regular parallel rows on all four sides of the
feeder and to each side of the stepped top
section as shown. When all of the mirrors
are in place and the glue is dry, wipe away
any fingerprints with a soft cloth.

Modernist Villa

This unusually shaped birdhouse pays homage to the modernist-style villas designed by Frank Lloyd Wright. Lloyd Wright was a master of his craft and was famous for making the best use of small spaces—but he never created a home this small! Large windows characterize this building style, so we've incorporated a transparent gallery on the side of the house that serves as an entranceway to the accommodation area.

You will need:

- basic tool kit (*see pages 8–11*)
- Modernist Villa template (*see page 169*)
- plain paper for templates
- one sheet ¹/₂-in. (12-mm)-thick plywood—2 x 4 ft (61 x 122 cm)
- approx. 10 x 12-in. (25.5 x 30.5-cm) sheet acrylic plastic from an old picture frame
- approx. 2-yd. (183-cm) length of ¹/₂ x ¹/₂-in. (12 x 12-mm)-square dowels for the gallery supports and exterior decoration
- wood glue
- approx. forty 1-in. (2.5-cm) paneling nails
- twenty-eight No. 2³/₈-in. (1.5 x 9.5-mm) countersunk brass screws for attaching gallery walls
- wood filler
- 40-oz. (1-l) can primer
- medium- and fine-grade sandpaper
- 40-oz. (1-l) cans of stone and dark brown latex-based exterior-grade paint
- household and artist's paintbrushes
- two 1¹/₂-in. (38-mm) brass flush hinges, plus fixing screws

First Steps | Trace and enlarge the templates provided on page 169 to full size;

then cut out the paper pattern pieces and transfer outlines to a sheet of ½-inch (12-mm)-thick plywood, marking any drill-hole positions with pencil dots. It may be helpful to indicate the positions of each dowel on the gallery template with pencil lines—see step 3. You may use this as a guide to positioning when carrying out step 5. Carefully

1

Apply the first coat of primer to the bare wooden surfaces. When the first coat is dry, sand it smooth using a fine-grade sandpaper; then apply a second coat, if necessary. Glue the front and back sections to the base as shown above, then turn the shape upside down in order to secure the pieces in place with paneling nails.

2

Turn the shape the right side up. Apply a bead of glue to both sides of the doorway section, and slot the shape into position between the back and front walls as shown above. Secure the doorway in place with paneling nails.

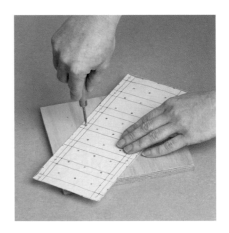

3

Using a utility knife and a ruler, cut two rectangular pieces of acrylic the same size as the gallery walls template provided on page 169. Place each piece in turn underneath the template and mark all the screw-hole positions using the point of an awl.

cut out the pieces using a jigsaw. Use a medium-grade sandpaper to smooth any rough or splintered edges. Drill a large hole in the position indicated on the decorative front section using the technique described in Basic Shape 1 (*see page 20*). Fill any voids that you may see along all four edges of each roof section. When they are dry, sand them smooth and wipe away any dust particles with a damp cloth.

4

Remove the template, and drill a hole through the acrylic at each of the previously marked screw-hole positions. Work carefully to avoid splitting the acrylic. To prevent the drill bit from slipping on the smooth surface, use the drill at a slow speed. You can also apply a strip of masking tape over the drill-hole positions to stop the point of the bit from sliding.

5

Using a small hacksaw, cut fourteen 4-inch (10-cm)-long pieces from ½ x ½-inch (12 x 12-mm)-square dowel. Sand the cut edges of each one smooth using a medium-grade sandpaper, then paint each one dark brown. Use small brass screws to secure seven lengths of dowel to the acrylic rectangles as shown above to form the transparent gallery walls.

6

Turn the main house shape upside down and position each gallery wall as shown above. Drill a pilot hole through the base of the gallery section into the ends of the square dowels. Insert a screw into each hole to secure the gallery wall in position. Secure the second wall in place in the same way, then turn the shape the right side up again.

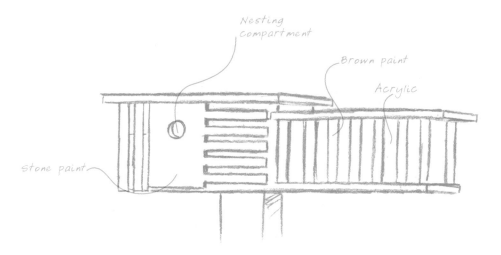

Nesting
Compartment

Brown paint

Acrylic

Stone paint

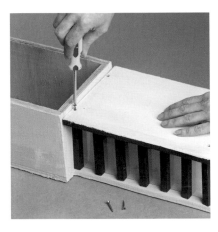

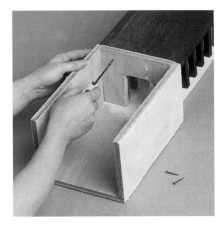

7

Apply two coats of primer to the gallery roof and, when dry, apply a coat of dark brown paint to the underside only. When the topcoat is dry, position the roof on the gallery as shown above. Drill a pilot hole through the roof down into the end dowel of each wall, then countersink the screw holes. Insert four screws to secure the roof in place.

8

Fill all four screw holes with wood filler using the flexible putty knife, then sand smooth when dry. Make sure that the surface of the gallery roof is completely flat before applying a topcoat of dark brown paint and allow it to dry. Examine the paint finish and apply a second coat, if necessary, to achieve a solid, even coverage.

9

Turn the box around so you can gain access to the interior. Measure and mark the position of the gallery roof on the inside walls. Mark and drill two pilot holes in the positions shown above, passing through the side wall and into the edge of the roof on the other side. Insert two screws to hold the gallery roof in place.

10

Apply a bead of glue along each side edge of the remaining wall section. Slide the section in place as shown, then nail it in place. Wipe away any excess glue with a damp cloth. Fill the joints with wood filler and sand it smooth when dry. Apply two thin layers of stone-colored paint to match the rest of the house and to complete the topcoat.

11

Cut two 5-inch (12.7-cm) and five 4¼-inch (10.5-cm) lengths of square dowel and sand the cut ends smooth. Paint the faux door section and all the dowels with dark brown paint. When the pieces are dry, glue them to the front of the house as shown. You should allow approximately ½ inch (12 mm) between each dowel. Use fine finishing nails to secure the faux door and the dowels to the front of the house.

12

Mark each screw-hole position for the brass hinges on the underside of the roof/lid and the top edge of the back wall with a pencil dot, then remove the hinges. Make a pilot hole at each pencil dot and screw the hinges to the box lid. Position the lid in place and secure the hinges to the top of the back wall as shown.

Diner

Do birds like hot dogs? Most wise little birds won't be fooled by the rooftop decoration on this mini diner, but they may be tempted by the bright colors of the exterior decorative paintwork to take a look inside. Hopefully the diner will provide a safe place for a nesting pair and its offspring for many seasons to come.

You will need:

- basic tool kit (*see pages 8–11*)

- Diner template (*see page 170*)

- plain paper for templates

- one sheet ½-in. (12-mm)-thick plywood— 2 x 4 ft (61 x 122 cm)

- 12-in. (30.5-cm) square of ¼-in. (6-mm)-thick plywood

- approx. 39-in. (1-m) length of 1-in. (2.5-cm)-wide concave molding for the awning

- approx. 36-in. (91.5-cm) length of 1⅜ x ⅛-in. (35 x 3-mm) strip wood for windows and door

- approx. 48-in. (122-cm) length of ¼-in. (6-mm)-square dowel for windowsills

- 5-in. (12.5-cm) length of ¾-in. (18-mm)-square dowel for sign supports

- wood glue

- approx. fifty 1-in. (2.5-cm) paneling nails

- approx. thirty 1-in. (2.5-cm) finishing nails

- approx. eighty 1-in. (2.5-cm) veneer nails

- four 1-in. (2.5-cm)-long wood screws

- wood filler

- 40-oz. (1-l) can primer

- medium- and fine-grade sandpaper

- 40-oz. (1-l) cans of emerald green, red, white, yellow, light green, orange, light beige, and brown latex-based exterior-grade paint

- household and artist's paintbrushes

- cotton swabs

- two 1½-in. (38-mm) brass flush hinges, plus fixing screws

- one 1-in. (2.5-cm) brass hanging bracket, plus fixing screws

First Steps | Trace and enlarge the templates provided on page 170 to full size; then cut out the paper pattern pieces and transfer the outlines to a sheet of ¹⁄₂-inch (12-mm)-thick and ¹⁄₄-inch (6-mm)-thick plywood as directed (see note on page 135 about the mitered sections). Be sure to mark any drill-hole positions with pencil dots. Carefully cut out the pieces using a jigsaw. Use a medium-grade sandpaper to smooth any

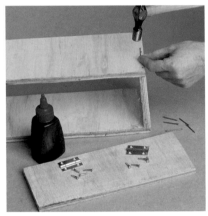

1

Apply a bead of wood glue to both of the outer edges of each side section, and position them between the front and back sections as shown above to form the basic rectangular box shape.

When the glue has set a little, turn the box on its back and then on its front to insert paneling nails to secure the joints. Wipe away any glue that may have seeped out with a damp cloth. Hinge and secure the base/access flap as described on pages 24–25.

2

Sit the box on the base; then apply a generous bead of glue along all four upper edges. Place the rectangular top section in place and secure it with paneling nails at approximately 2-inch (5-cm) intervals.

Wipe away excess glue using a damp cloth. When the glue is completely dry, use a piece of sandpaper to smooth the edges of the top section so they lie perfectly flush with the side walls.

3

For the awning, hold the first piece of molding in position against the top front edge. Mark the position of the box corners along the top edge of the molding with pencil dots, then indicate the direction of the miter cut.

Cut the molding to size, then fix temporarily in place with masking tape. Do the same with the back section, then measure and cut each side piece to fit. It is best to measure and cut each piece individually to achieve a good fit. Sand all cut edges smooth.

rough or splintered edges. Drill an access hole where indicated on one side section using the technique described for Basic Shape 1 (*see page 20*), and sand the cut edges smooth.

NOTE

There are no templates or measurements supplied for the mitered sections that form the awning. It is far easier to take the measurement directly from the diner—you will achieve a better and more accurate fit. Practice using the miter saw on a spare piece of narrow lumber before cutting the molding to avoid mistakes.

4

Remove the tape and apply a generous bead of glue to the back of each piece of molding and along the mitered edge. Position it on the box and make sure that the angled edges meet neatly.

Secure the front and back sections first; then glue the sides in place. If you find that the corners do not meet correctly, sand them down a little to achieve a better fit. Allow the glue to dry a little, then use finishing nails to hold the molding in place.

5

Fill all joints and voids with wood filler, then sand smooth when dry. Wipe away any dust particles with a damp cloth before applying two coats of primer. Sand the surface smooth using a fine-grade sandpaper between coats. When the primer is dry, apply a coat of white paint to the awning only.

6

Mark the striped pattern on the awning using a ½-inch (12-mm)-wide strip of paper as a template. Indicate the center of the awning pieces of all four sides with pencil dots then mark the parallel stripes using the strip of paper as a guide, working outward from the pencil mark. Because the molding is curved, it is difficult to use a ruler for this step.

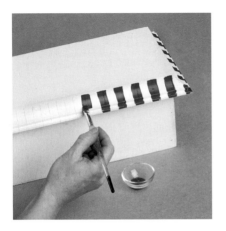

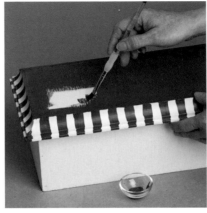

7

Using a small artist's paintbrush, paint each alternate stripe red on all four sections of the awning. Take your time to carefully follow the pencil lines. Begin at one corner and work your way around all four sides so you do not smudge the wet paint with your hands as you go. Allow the red paint to dry and apply a second coat, if necessary.

8

Apply a thin coat of red paint to the roof of the diner. Allow the paint to dry, then examine the finish. If it looks a little patchy, apply a second coat. It is always better to apply two thin layers of paint than one thick one.

9

When the roof of the diner has dried, apply emerald green paint to the walls. Dark shades of paint often require a second or a third coat to achieve an even, solid color coverage.

Hot dog:
brown paint

Sign

Bun:
light beige paint

Canopy:
red and white paint

Entry to nesting
compartment

Windows with
flower boxes

Emerald
green paint

10

Using a small hacksaw or miter saw, cut one 3½-inch (9-cm)-long door piece, and sixteen 2-inch (5-cm)-long window pieces. For the windowsills, cut two 5-inch (12.5-cm) and two 9¾-inch (24.75-cm) lengths of ¼-inch (6-mm)-square dowel.

Sand all cut edges smooth. Paint all of the windows white, and the doors and the windowsills red. When the white paint on the windows is dry, add a narrow frame of red paint to the side and top edge of each one.

11

Using the tip of a cotton swab, apply thick spots of light green paint at the lower edge of each window to simulate foliage. When the green paint is dry, apply spots of red, yellow, and orange to represent flowers. Finally, using a small artist's paintbrush, apply a tiny spot of a contrast color to the center of each flower.

12

Apply glue to the back of the door and position it on the left side of the front as shown above. Glue the short windowsill pieces to each end of the box, and the longer ones to the back and the front—each about 1¼ inch (3 cm) up from the lower edge of the diner.

Glue six windows to the front, five to the back, three to the right end, and two to the left end of the box on both sides of the entrance hole. When all of the glue is dry, secure the pieces in place with fine finishing nails.

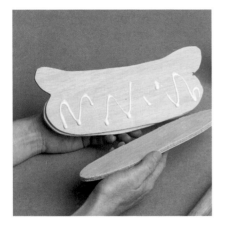

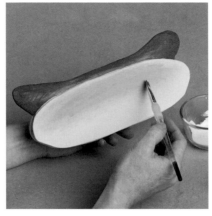

13

Glue together the two oval "bun" shapes and the hot dog center section as shown above. Squeeze the three layers together and wipe away any glue that may seep out from the edges with a damp cloth. Once the glue has dried, use a few short veneer nails to secure the shapes together.

14

Apply a coat of primer, then when dry, apply a base coat of light beige to the two halves of the "bun." Paint the hot dog brown, then add highlights and shading to both when the base coats are dry—using the picture as a guide. Apply a coat of primer and one or two base coats of yellow paint to the sign section, then allow it to dry.

15

Cut one 2-inch (5-cm) and one 3-inch (7.5-cm)-long pieces of ½-inch (12-mm) square dowel for the sign and hot dog supports. Drill two pilot holes through each one about ½ inch (12 mm) from both ends, then countersink each drill hole. Paint both support blocks red. Trace the "Eat Here" text given on page 170, then transfer the outlines of each letter to the plywood shape.

16

Using a fine artist's paintbrush and red paint, carefully fill in each letter of the "Eat Here" sign. These letters are quite fine and it requires a steady hand to achieve a good result. If you are not confident in your painting skills, you could use a fine red permanent marker to fill in the letters instead.

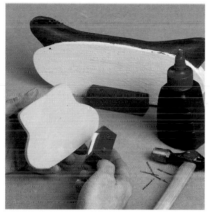

17

Apply a generous bead of glue to one side of the fixing blocks, then place the shorter one on the back of the sign and the longer of the two on the back of the hot dog shape. When the glue is dry, lay the sign and the hot dog flat on your work surface. Drive two paneling nails through the front of the sign and the hot dog to secure to the blocks underneath.

18

Place the hot dog and sign on the top of the diner and indicate the position of the fixing blocks on the roof using pencil dots. Remove the signs and apply a bead of glue to the underside of each block before replacing them. When the glue has dried a little, insert a screw into each of the predrilled and countersunk holes in order to secure the blocks to the roof.

Bandstand Feeder

This feeder was inspired by an old photograph of a bandstand in a park in Jonesborough, Tennessee. The pretty octagonal shape is typical of these structures and although the design requires careful drilling and measuring, the construction isn't as difficult as it looks. The bandstand may be mounted on a pole, secured in a large tree, or hung from a sturdy branch if a screw eye is inserted into the top.

You will need:

- basic tool kit (*see pages 8–11*)
- Bandstand Feeder template (*see page 171*)
- plain paper for templates
- one sheet ½-in. (12-mm)-thick plywood—2 x 4 ft (61 x 122 cm)
- 6-in. (15-cm) length of 1-in. (2.5-cm)-diameter dowel for roof support
- 6-ft (183-cm) length of ½-in. (12-mm)-diameter dowel for side supports
- 36-in. (91.5-cm) length of decorative quarter-round molding
- wood glue
- sixteen 1½-in. (38-cm)-long wood screws
- one ½-in. (12-mm)-long domed wood screw or screw eye for hanging
- approx. twenty 1-in. (2.5-cm) paneling nails
- wood filler
- 40-oz. (1-l) can primer

- medium- and fine-grade sandpaper
- one sheet 18-in. (46-cm)-square thin aluminum
- approx. 2-in. (5-cm)-diameter fluted tart pan
- 40-oz. (1-l) cans of antique cream and red latex-based exterior-grade paint
- small dish for bird feed
- one can of red spray paint
- household and artist's paintbrushes
- pop riveting tool, plus two rivets

First Steps | Trace and enlarge the templates provided on page 171 to full size;
then cut out the paper pattern pieces and transfer the outlines to a sheet of ½-inch
(12-mm)-thick plywood. Be sure to accurately mark any drill-hole positions with pencil
dots. Carefully cut out the pieces using a jigsaw. Use a medium-grade sandpaper to
smooth any rough or splintered edges.

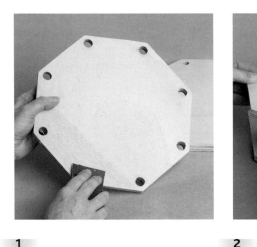

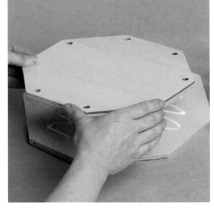

1

Take the two smaller octagonal shapes
and drill eight holes where they are
indicated on the template. Use a spade
bit that matches the diameter of the
narrower dowel. It is important that
these holes are positioned accurately on
both pieces. Sand any rough or splintered
edges with a medium-grade sandpaper.

2

Apply a generous amount of wood glue
to the larger octagonal piece; then place
one of the smaller pieces on top as shown.
This design allows a margin of about ½
inch (12 mm) to form a neat step.

While the glue is still wet, make sure
that the margin is equal all around. Secure
the pieces with paneling nails. Wipe away
any glue that may have seeped out from
around the edges with a damp cloth.
Set the pieces aside to allow the glue
to dry completely.

3

Using a small hacksaw, cut eight 6½-
inch (16.5-cm)-long pieces of ½-inch
(12-mm)-diameter dowel, then sand all
of the cut edges smooth. Lay one of the
octagonal sections on your work surface
and squeeze a small amount of wood
glue into each of the predrilled holes.

Place a dowel into each hole, then
secure it in place with a hammer. Wipe
away excess glue with a damp cloth. This
section forms the base of the bandstand.

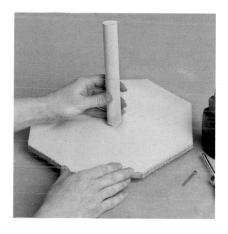

4

Cut a 7-inch (18-cm) length of the thicker dowel and glue it to the center of the remaining octagonal section. This will form the support for the metal roof. When the glue has dried, drill a pilot hole into the base of the dowel from the underside of the shape. Insert a long wood screw to hold the support securely in place. This piece forms the roof of the bandstand.

5

Squeeze a small amount of glue into each predrilled hole on the underside of the roof section, then place it onto the base, making sure that each of the dowel supports connects with a hole. Drill a pilot hole through the roof into each dowel, and insert a wood screw to secure it in place. Do the same to secure the bottom end of the dowels to the base of the bandstand.

6

Fill all voids with wood filler, then sand smooth when dry. Wipe away any dust particles with a damp cloth before applying two coats of primer. Sand the shape smooth using a fine-grade sandpaper between coats. Using a miter saw, cut the the quarter-round molding to fit the step around the edge of the roof section. The angle of the cut edge should be about $22\frac{1}{2}$ degrees. Sand all of the cut edges smooth.

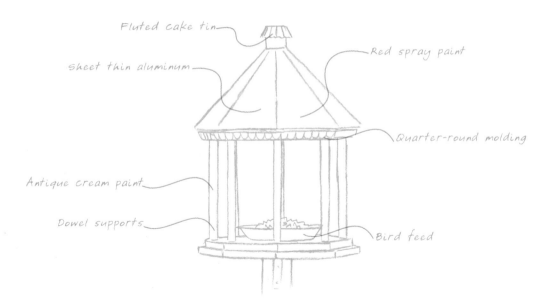

Fluted cake tin

Sheet thin aluminum

Red spray paint

Quarter-round molding

Antique cream paint

Dowel supports

Bird feed

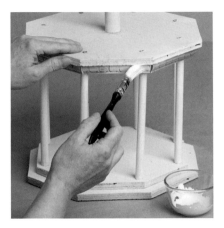

7

Apply a bead of wood glue to the back of each mitered section and place each one in position along the step at the edge of the roof section. If your cuts are accurate, the pieces should fit neatly together, but you can sand the edges a little to adjust the fit, if necessary. When the glue is dry, secure the pieces in place with fine finishing nails on either side of the miter at each corner.

8

Apply the first base coat of the antique cream paint, stippling the paintbrush bristles into the molded details to ensure an even paint coverage. Apply a second coat, if necessary. Allow the paint to dry completely before applying the other decorative details.

9

Using a small artist's brush, apply red paint to the stepped edges of the base and roof section. When the first coat is dry, apply a second to provide an even coverage.

If you intend to hang the bandstand from a tree, apply red paint to the underside of the base. Using a small dry paintbrush, apply a small amount of red paint very lightly over the surface of the decorative molding to accentuate the pattern.

10

Trace the outline of the roof section onto the sheet of thin aluminum. Do not remove the protective plastic layer yet. Copy the fold lines and fixing tab cutting lines at the center of the roof. Cut along the outside edge, and into the fixing tabs at the center. Cut a 2 ½ x 1-inch (6.35 x 2.5-cm) band from the aluminum, too.

11

Place your metal ruler on each of the fold lines and bend the metal carefully—this will form the three-dimensional-rooftop shape that sits on the bandstand. Peel away the protective plastic layer.

HINTS AND SUGGESTIONS

• *Always use spray paints in a well-ventilated area or preferably outside. Cover surrounding surfaces with newspaper to protect them from spray "fall out" in the air. Don't use spray paint on a windy day!*

• *A metal dish can be placed inside the bandstand to hold seeds and other treats.*

• *You can use the red spray paint to decorate the dish to match the roof and, as an added precaution, drill a hole through the base of the dish and screw it securely to the inside of the bandstand.*

12

Place the rooftop, the band, and the small tart pan on a sheet of newspaper and apply a thin coat of glossy red spray paint. Allow the first coat to dry, then add another, if necessary. It is best to apply two thin coats than one thick one because spray paint can easily run and drip—spoiling the finish.

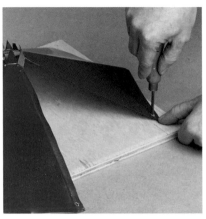

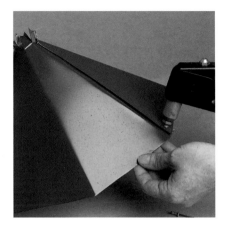

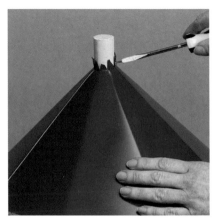

13

Pierce four large holes through the metal where indicated on the overlap part. These should be large enough to accommodate the shaft of the rivet that will hold the metal edges together.

14

Overlap the metal and match up the holes, insert the rivet, and use the riveting tool to make the joint secure. Insert a fixing rivet through the holes at the top edge in the same way.

15

Using the awl, pierce a hole through two of the tabs at the center of the roof and into the dowel support. Insert a small screw to hold the roof to the dowel support.

SEEDS AND FOOD PREFERENCES

There are hundreds of bird species and they all have different food preferences. Birds are also fickle and can change their minds according to climate conditions and the availability of natural foods. Trial and error is the order of the day— experiment a little with various combinations until you find the one that your local bird visitors prefer. Here are a few examples:

Black-oil sunflower seeds:
cardinals, chickadees, finches, flickers, jays, sparrows, titmice

Seed mixes:
goldfinches, robins, nuthatches, sparrows, thrushes, titmice, woodpeckers, wrens, doves

Peanuts, nut mixes:
sparrows, chickadees, titmice, cardinals

Millet/corn:
doves

Fruit/dried fruit/berries
cardinals, buntings, chickadees, goldfinches, jays, tanagers, thrushes, bluebirds, warblers, wrens

Suet/peanut butter mixes:
jays, mockingbirds, robins, nuthatches, sparrows, titmice, woodpeckers, wrens

Kitchen scraps
jays, mockingbirds, robins, sparrows, thrushes

Seed mixes should include: black-oil sunflower seeds, striped sunflower seeds, peanuts, millet, corn, thistle seeds (nyjer), and safflower seeds.

16

Wrap the band around the top of the dowel support and neatly overlap the edges. Using the awl, pierce a small hole through both layers of metal at the overlap and into the dowel underneath.

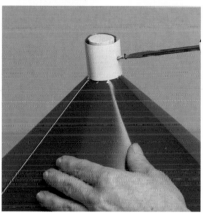

17

Insert a small screw into the hole to hold the band to the dowel support.

18

Using the awl, pierce a hole though the center of the small tart pan. Place it on top of the dowel support; then pierce a pilot hole into the dowel underneath. Insert a small fixing screw to hold the pan in place.

If you intend to hang the bandstand from a tree, insert a large screw eye instead.

Paddle Steamer

One look at this colorful paddle steamer will surely have all the birds visiting your garden chirping songs from *Showboat*! The shaped galleries and decks are cutouts fixed to a basic rectangular box that forms the central accommodation space. The colorful decorative paint effects allow plenty of opportunities for artistic expression. Use our picture as a guide, or try to include your own designs and patterns to add a personal touch.

You will need:

- basic tool kit (*see pages 8–11*)
- Paddle Steamer template (*see pages 172–173*)
- plain paper for templates
- two sheets 1/2-in. (12-mm)-thick plywood—2 x 4 ft (61 x 122 cm)
- half sheet 1/4-in. (6-mm)-thick plywood—2 x 2 ft (61 x 61 cm)
- two 10-in. (25.5-cm) lengths of 1 1/8-in. (2.8-cm)-diameter dowel for funnels
- 12-in. (30.5-cm) length of 3/8-in. (9-mm)-diameter dowel for flagpole
- wood glue
- approx. one hundred 1-in. (2.5-cm) paneling nails
- wood filler
- nine 1 1/2-in. (38-mm)-long wood screws
- 40-oz. (1-l) can primer
- medium- and fine-grade sandpaper

- cotton swabs
- small piece thin aluminum (the side of a can) or thin sheet of aluminum
- 40-oz. (1-l) cans of yellow, red, and blue latex-based exterior-grade paint
- household and artist's paintbrushes
- two 1 1/2-in. (38-mm) brass flush hinges, plus fixing screws
- one 1-in. (2.5-cm) brass turn button, plus fixing screws

First Steps | Trace and enlarge the templates provided on pages 172–173 to full size; then cut out the paper pattern pieces and transfer the outlines to a sheet of ½-inch-(12 mm)-thick and ¼-inch (6-mm)-thick plywood and thin aluminum as directed. Mark any drill-hole positions with pencil dots. Carefully cut out the pieces using a jigsaw. For the gallery arches, use a finer scroll blade in your jigsaw, which will enable you to cut

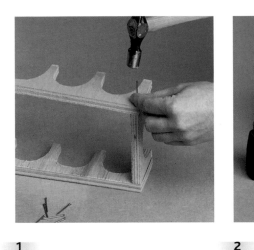

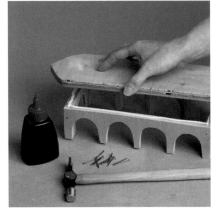

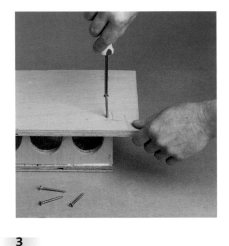

1

Gather the four upper gallery sections together for assembly. Apply a bead of glue along both side edges of the shorter front and back pieces. Position them between the two longer side sections as shown.

When the glue has set a little, turn the shape on its side and drive in paneling nails to secure the joints at each end as shown above. Do the same on the other side.

2

Stand the gallery on your work surface as shown above and apply a bead of glue along all four upper edges. Position the gallery rooftop in place; then insert paneling nails through the roof and down into the side walls at intervals of about 2 inches (5 cm) to secure it in place. Wipe away any glue that may seep out with a damp cloth.

3

Turn the upper gallery upside down and position the roof of the main accommodation compartment on top, making sure that the drill-hole positions align correctly with the gallery corners.

Drill a pilot hole through the roof section and down into the gallery walls underneath. Insert a screw into each hole to secure the roof to the gallery.

around the tight, curved shapes. Use a medium-grade sandpaper to smooth any rough or splintered edges. Drill an access hole in the position indicated on the side section using the technique described for Basic Shape 1 (*see page 20*), and sand the cut edges smooth. Wipe away all dust particles with a damp cloth. This will be a time-consuming process because there are many straight and curved cut edges in this design.

4

Take the front wall and both side walls of the accommodation section. Apply a bead of wood glue along both sides of the shorter front piece. Position it between the two side walls. When the glue has set a little, turn the shape on its side to drive in paneling nails at each end. Do the same on the other side.

5

Stand the shape on your work surface the right side up as shown. Apply a bead of wood glue along the edge of all three sides. Position the upper gallery onto the side walls and use paneling nails to secure it in place. Refer to the dotted positioning lines on your templates for accurate placement.

6

Turn the shape upside down to secure the deck section. Apply a generous bead of glue around the three edges of the main accommodation compartment; then position the deck in place using the template as a guide.

Drill and countersink pilot holes where indicated and insert a screw into each hole. Note that the two top deck/hull layers have straight sides, while the lower hull section has an angled edge.

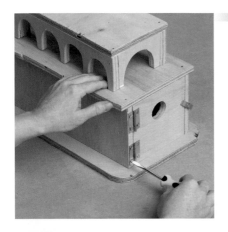

7

Check the fit of the rear access door. Sand the edges for a snug fit. Mark the position of the two hinges on the left side and indicate the screw hole on the door and side wall with pencil dots.

Remove the door and make pilot holes at each dot. Screw the hinges to the door, then replace the door in position. Secure the hinges to the side wall, then screw a turn button to the right side wall.

8

Apply wood glue to the back of the three arched lower deck walls. Position the longer side sections onto the accommodation compartment first, then position the shorter front end. When the glue has dried, secure the shaped pieces using paneling nails.

9

Take the three upper deck walls and add them to the main compartment in the same way as before. Secure the deck walls in place using paneling nails; then wipe away any excess glue with a damp cloth.

ALL BIRDS ON DECK

The Paddle Steamer birdhouse isn't a feeder as such, but the upper gallery provides a handy space for a few tasty morsels that may attract a breeding pair, and if they like what they see, they may decide to take up residence. Try threading some small pieces of fruit onto a piece of string, place it inside the gallery, and then secure the ends to the arches so the birds can't make off with the whole thing!

10

Turn the shape upside down again to secure the remaining hull sections. Apply a generous amount of glue to the underside of the deck section, then place the next deck/hull section on top of it, making sure that the outer edges match. Press the shape down firmly and wipe away any excess glue with a damp cloth.

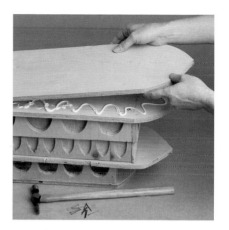

11

Apply the last hull section—the one with the angled outer edge—in place in the same way. Secure the layers together with paneling nails. You can also use screws, if you prefer. Drill pilot holes at intervals around the edge of the hull, then countersink each one. Insert a screw into each hole to secure the layers together. Fill the screw holes with wood filler, then sand smooth when dry.

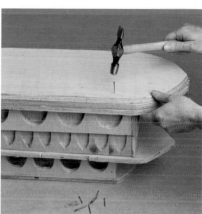

12

Fill all joints and voids with wood filler and sand smooth when dry. Wipe away any dust particles with a damp cloth before applying the two coats of primer. Sand the shape smooth with a fine-grade sandpaper between coats.

HINTS AND SUGGESTIONS

• *If you don't have a steady hand and are a little unsure of your painting skills, you may find it easier to prime the upper and lower deck walls before attachment. In this case, you will also need to prime and paint the walls of the main shape yellow. This will provide neat, clean paint lines around the arches.*

• *As an alternative to metal, you can use small pieces of plastic cut from the side of a soda bottle for the flag and the funnel tops. Simply cut out following the template provided on page 172 and spray it with blue paint.*

Flagpole

Funnel

Funnel Covers

Yellow paint

Red paint

Decorative paddle Cover

Blue paint

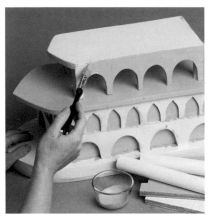

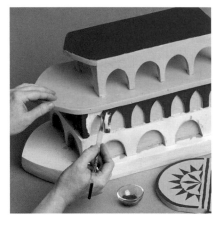

13

Apply a coat of yellow paint to the upper gallery and roof, the roof of the accommodation compartment, inside the arches of the upper and lower decks, the flagpole, and the semicircular paddle covers. Allow the paint to dry before applying a second coat, if necessary.

Use the template on page 172 to trace the decorative pattern on both paddle covers with faint pencil lines.

14

Apply a coat of red paint to the upper gallery rooftop, the arched walls of the upper deck, both funnels, and sections of the decorative pattern on the paddle covers. Allow the paint to dry, then apply a second coat, if necessary.

15

To complete the decorative base coats, apply blue paint to the arched walls of the lower deck, the deck, the funnel tops, the flag, the hull, and the remaining details on the paddle covers.

16

Glue the paddle covers and funnels in place. Allow the glue to dry completely; then use paneling nails to secure the semicircular covers. For the funnels, you will need to adopt a slightly different approach: Hammer a nail at an angle through the base of each funnel into the roof/deck below.

17

Wrap the flag around the top of the flagpole and secure with a small veneer nail. Pass the flagpole through the hole drilled though the roof in the position indicated on the pattern template. Make sure that the drill-hole diameter matches the diameter of the flagpole.

18

Use a cotton swab to apply spots of color in rows around the rooftop edges and the curved arches of the gallery and decks. Use the photograph on page 149 as a guide and apply other decorative flourishes with a small artist's brush. There are no hard-and-fast rules here—you can use your imagination.

Templates: basic shapes

BASIC SHAPE 1 PAGE 20

Templates are 25 percent of actual size—enlarge by
400 percent for full-size template (*see page 7
for copying instructions*).

SIDE
cut 2

ROOF
cut 1

cut to 30° angle (approx.)

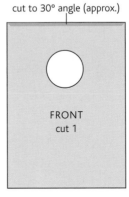

FRONT
cut 1

cut to 30° angle (approx.)

BACK
cut 1

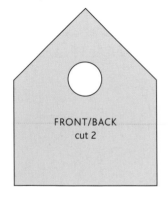

BASE
cut 1

BASIC SHAPE 2 PAGE 22

Templates are 25 percent of actual size—
enlarge by 400 percent for full-size template
(*see page 7 for copying instructions*).

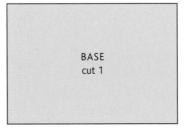

BASE
cut 1

FRONT/BACK
cut 2

ROOF
cut 1

Apex

ROOF
cut 1

Apex

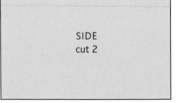

SIDE
cut 2

BASIC SHAPE 3 PAGE 24

Templates are 25 percent of actual size—enlarge by 400 percent for full-size template (*see page 7 for copying instructions*).

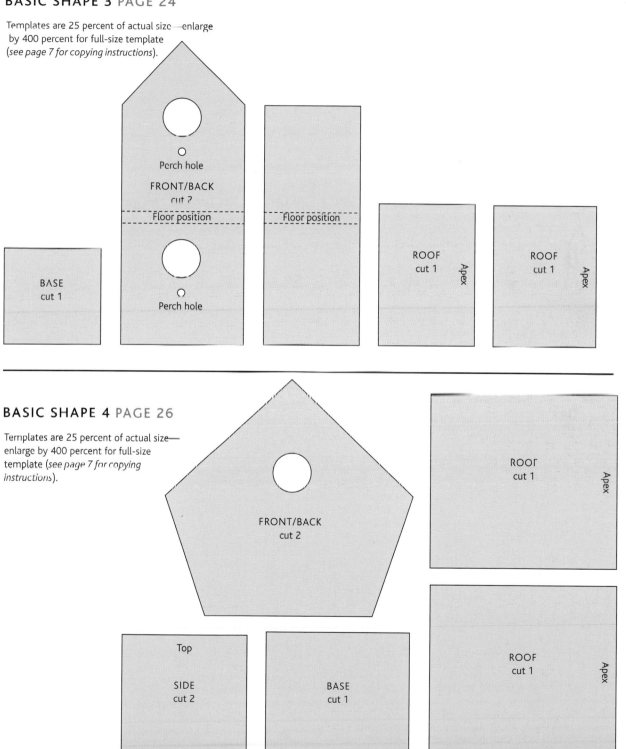

Perch hole

FRONT/BACK
cut 2

Floor position

Floor position

ROOF
cut 1

Apex

ROOF
cut 1

Apex

BASE
cut 1

Perch hole

BASIC SHAPE 4 PAGE 26

Templates are 25 percent of actual size—enlarge by 400 percent for full-size template (*see page 7 for copying instructions*).

FRONT/BACK
cut 2

ROOF
cut 1

Apex

Top

SIDE
cut 2

BASE
cut 1

ROOF
cut 1

Apex

Templates: projects

BEACH CABANA PAGE 30

Templates are 25 percent of actual size—enlarge by 400 percent for full-size template
(*see page 7 for copying instructions*). This is an extended Basic Shape 1.

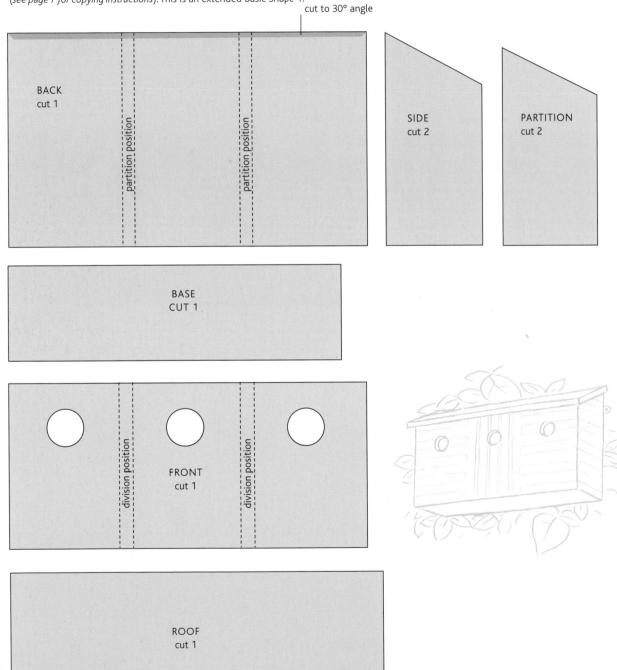

cut to 30° angle

BACK
cut 1

partition position

partition position

SIDE
cut 2

PARTITION
cut 2

BASE
CUT 1

division position

division position

FRONT
cut 1

ROOF
cut 1

GINGERBREAD COTTAGE PAGE 36

Templates are 50 percent of actual size—enlarge by 200 percent for full-size template (*see page 7 for copying instructions*). Use Basic Shape 2.

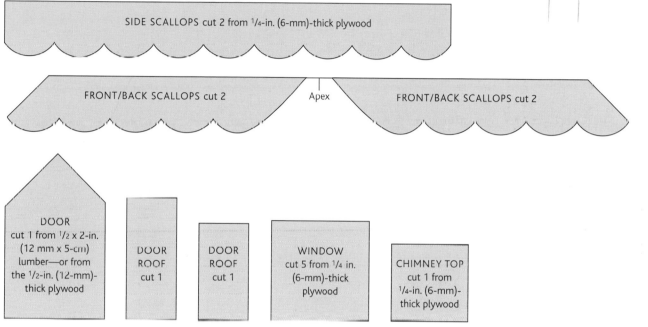

SIDE SCALLOPS cut 2 from ¼-in. (6-mm)-thick plywood

FRONT/BACK SCALLOPS cut 2   Apex   FRONT/BACK SCALLOPS cut 2

DOOR
cut 1 from ½ x 2-in.
(12 mm x 5-cm)
lumber—or from
the ½-in. (12-mm)-
thick plywood

DOOR
ROOF
cut 1

DOOR
ROOF
cut 1

WINDOW
cut 5 from ¼ in.
(6-mm)-thick
plywood

CHIMNEY TOP
cut 1 from
¼-in. (6-mm)-
thick plywood

LOG CABIN PAGE 42

Templates are 25 percent of actual size—enlarge by 400 percent for full-size template (*see page 7 for copying instructions*). Use Basic Shape 2 with trimmed roof.

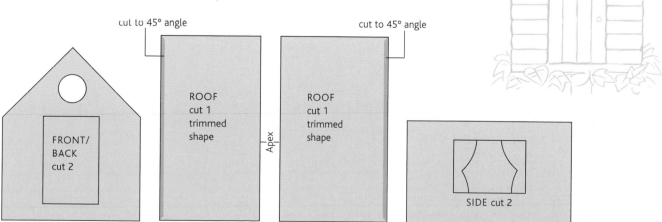

cut to 45° angle   cut to 45° angle

FRONT/
BACK
cut 2

ROOF
cut 1
trimmed
shape

Apex

ROOF
cut 1
trimmed
shape

SIDE cut 2

Templates: projects

CHURCH PAGE 48

Templates are 100 percent of actual size. Use Basic Shape 2.

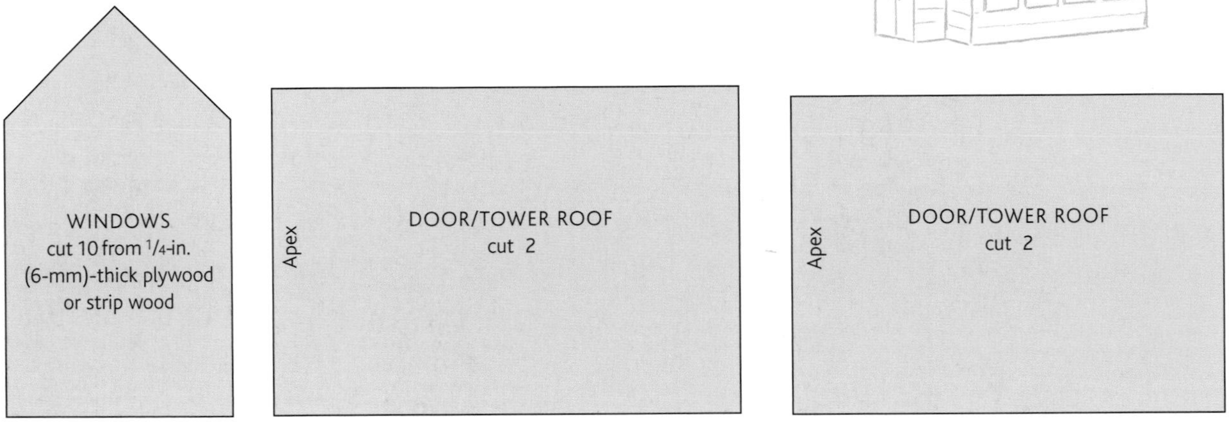

WINDOWS
cut 10 from $\frac{1}{4}$-in.
(6-mm)-thick plywood
or strip wood

Apex

DOOR/TOWER ROOF
cut 2

Apex

DOOR/TOWER ROOF
cut 2

CINDERELLA'S CASTLE PAGE 54

Templates are 25 percent of actual size—enlarge by 400 percent for full-size template. (*see page 7 for copying instructions*). Use Basic Shape 2 with trimmed roof and battlements.

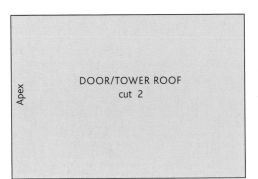

cut to 45° angle

cut to 45° angle

ROOF
cut 1
trimmed shape

Apex

ROOF
cut 1
trimmed shape

Apex

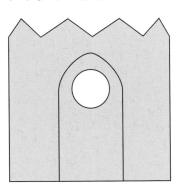

BATTLEMENTS FRONT/BACK
cut 2 from $\frac{1}{4}$-in. (6-mm)-thick
plywood

**TOWER
CUTTING
TEMPLATE**

**TOWER
CUTTING TEMPLATE**

**PAINTING DETAIL
TEMPLATE FOR TOWERS
AND SIDE WINDOWS**

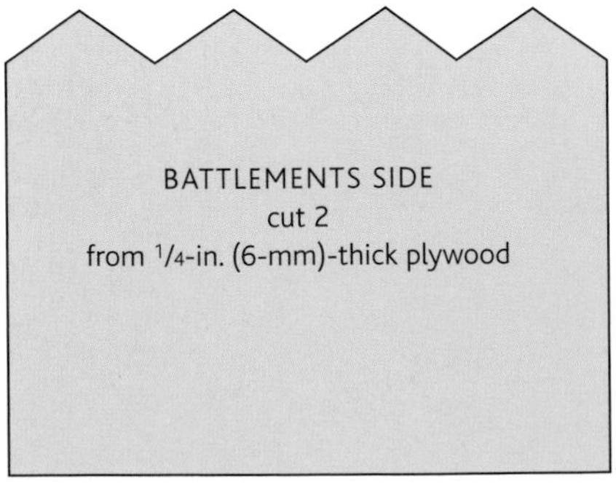

BATTLEMENTS SIDE
cut 2
from $\frac{1}{4}$-in. (6-mm)-thick plywood

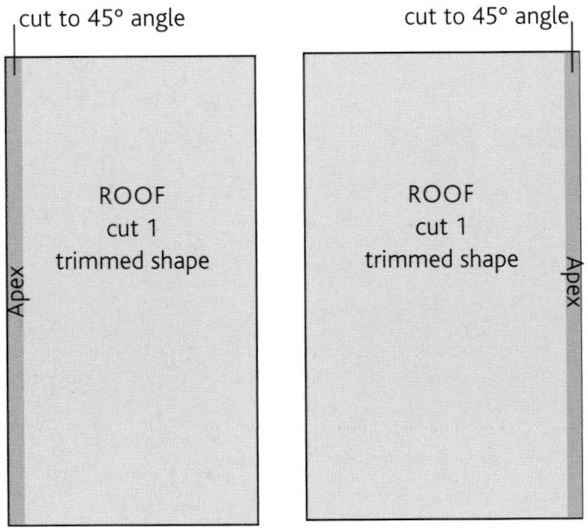

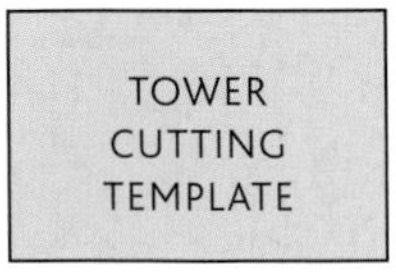

HAUNTED HOUSE PAGE 60

Templates are 33 percent of actual size—enlarge by 300 percent for full-size template (*see page 7 for copying instructions*). This is a customized Basic Shape 3.

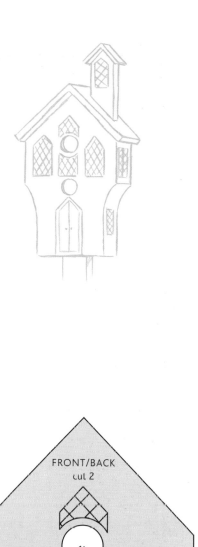

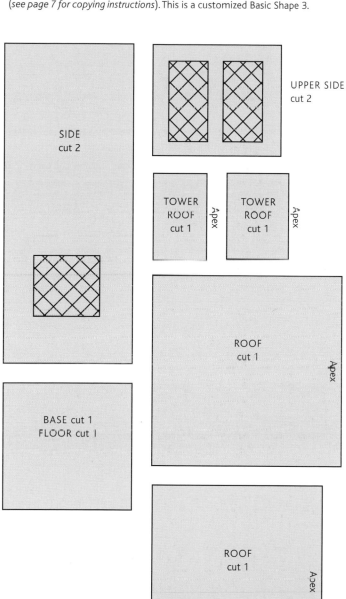

SIDE
cut 2

UPPER SIDE
cut 2

TOWER
ROOF
cut 1

Apex

TOWER
ROOF
cut 1

Apex

BASE cut 1
FLOOR cut 1

ROOF
cut 1

Apex

ROOF
cut 1

Apex

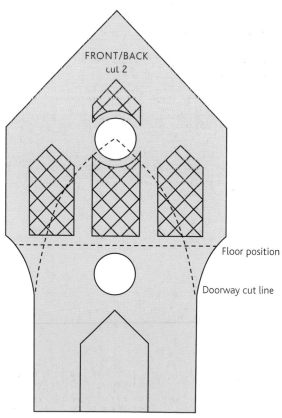

FRONT/BACK
cut 2

Floor position

Doorway cut line

Templates: projects

SWISS CHALET PAGE 66

Templates are 100 percent of actual size.
Use Basic Shape 4.

DOOR ROOF
cut 1

Apex

DOOR ROOF
cut 1

Apex

SHUTTERS
cut 4 from
strip wood

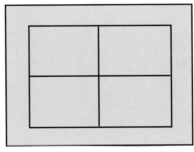

WINDOW
cut 2 from ¹/₄-in. (6-mm)-thick plywood

DOOR
cut 1

NEOCLASSICAL TEMPLE PAGE 72

Templates are 50 percent of actual size—enlarge by 200 percent
for full-size template (*see page 7 for copying instructions*).

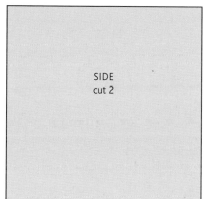

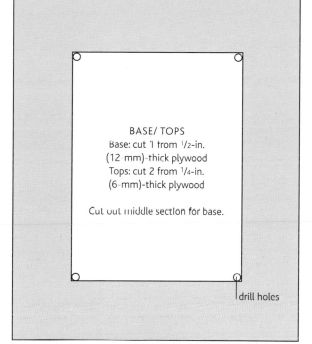

BASE/ TOPS
Base: cut 1 from 1/2-in.
(12-mm)-thick plywood
Tops: cut 2 from 1/4-in.
(6-mm)-thick plywood

Cut out middle section for base.

drill holes

SIDE
cut 2

TRIANGULAR
ROOF SUPPORT
cut 2

cut to 20° angle

ROOF
cut 2

Apex

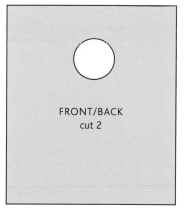

FRONT/BACK
cut 2

BASE
cut 1

Templates: projects

SANDCASTLE PAGE 78

Templates are 25 percent of actual size—enlarge by 400 percent for full-size template (*see page 7 for copying instructions*).

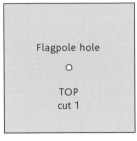

Flagpole hole

○

TOP
cut 1

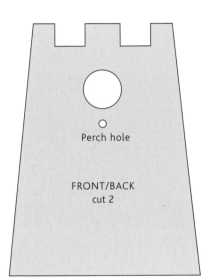

○
Perch hole

FRONT/BACK
cut 2

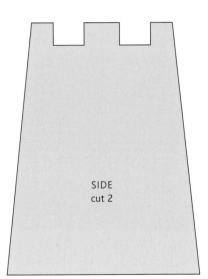

SIDE
cut 2

BASE
cut 1

PYRAMID PAGE 84

Templates are 25 percent of actual size—enlarge by 400 percent for full-size template (*see page 7 for copying instructions*).

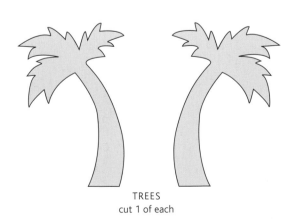

TREES
cut 1 of each

BASE
cut 1
cut out middle section

SPACE ROCKET PAGE 90

Templates are 25 percent of actual size—enlarge by 400 percent for full-size template (*see page 7 for copying instructions*).

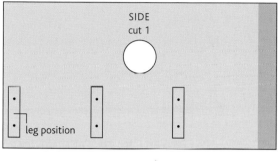

SIDE
cut 1

leg position

LEG
cut 3

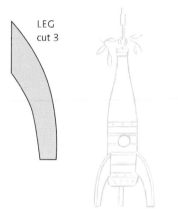

TEA PARTY FEEDER PAGE 96

Templates are 20 percent of actual size—enlarge by 500 percent (or by 250 percent, then by 200 percent) for full-size template (*see page 7 for copying instructions*).

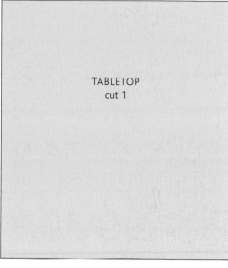

TABLETOP
cut 1

TABLE SIDES
cut 4

BASE/FLAP
cut 1

back edge—cut to 45-degree angle

ROOF
cut 1

SIDE
cut 4

cut all edges to approx.
45-degree angle

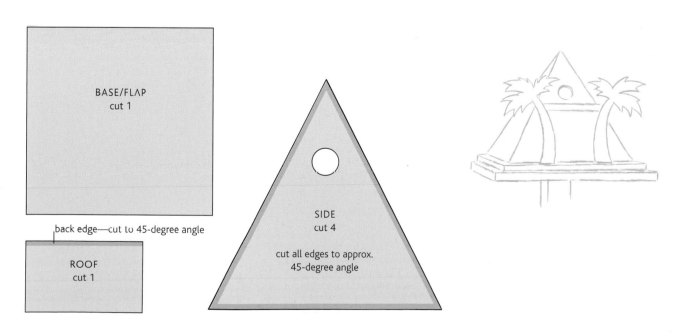

Templates: projects

SWIMMING POOL FEEDER PAGE 102

Templates are 25 percent of actual size—enlarge by 400 percent for full-size template (*see page 7 for copying instructions*).

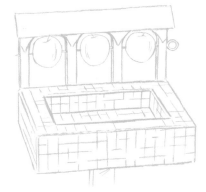

APPLE FEEDER ARCHES cut 1 from ¼-in. (6-mm)-thick plywood

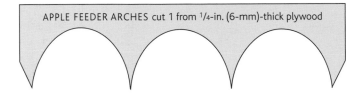

POOL FRONT/BACK
cut 2

POOL SIDE
cut 2

FEEDER ROOF
cut 1 from ¼-in. (6-mm)-thick plywood

POOL TOP/BASE
cut 1 wIth window
cut 1 without

POOL WATER
CONTAINER SIDE
cut 2

POOL WATER CONTAINER FRONT/BACK
cut 2

TOWER FEEDER PAGE 108

Templates are 25 percent of actual size—enlarge by 400 percent for full-size template (*see page 7 for copying instructions*).

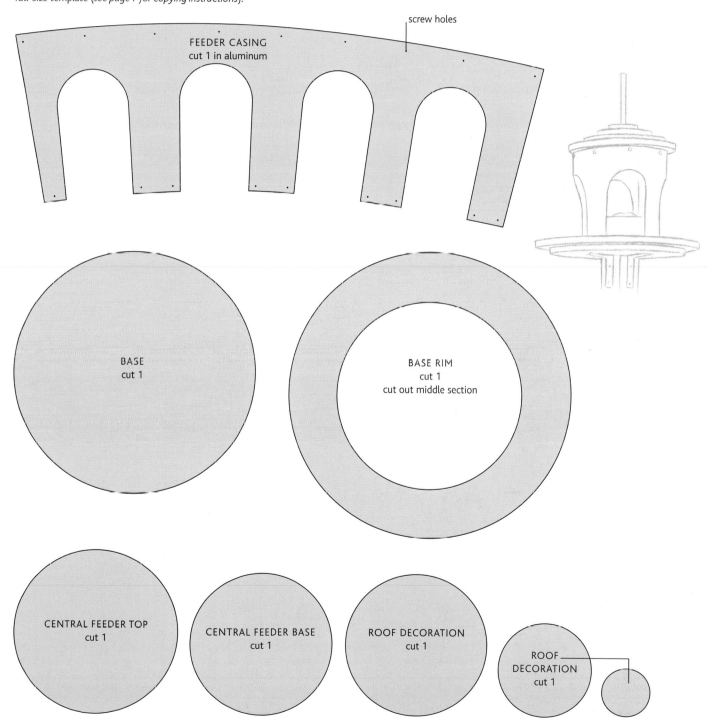

screw holes

FEEDER CASING
cut 1 in aluminum

BASE
cut 1

BASE RIM
cut 1
cut out middle section

CENTRAL FEEDER TOP
cut 1

CENTRAL FEEDER BASE
cut 1

ROOF DECORATION
cut 1

ROOF DECORATION
cut 1

Templates: projects

MEDITERRANEAN FEEDER PAGE 114

Templates are 25 percent of actual size—enlarge by 400 percent for full-size template (*see page 7 for copying instructions*).

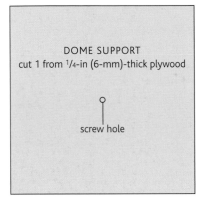

DOME SUPPORT
cut 1 from 1/4-in (6-mm)-thick plywood

screw hole

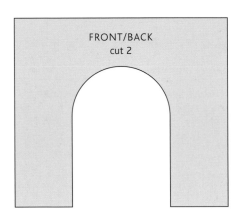

FRONT/BACK
cut 2

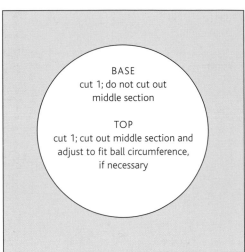

BASE
cut 1; do not cut out middle section

TOP
cut 1; cut out middle section and adjust to fit ball circumference, if necessary

SIDE
cut 2

HIGH-RISE FEEDER PAGE 120

Templates are 25 percent of actual size—enlarge by 400 percent for full-size template (*see page 7 for copying instructions*).

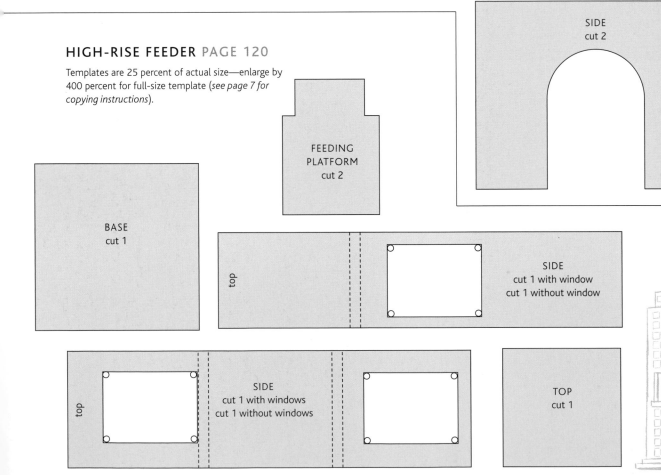

FEEDING PLATFORM
cut 2

BASE
cut 1

top

SIDE
cut 1 with window
cut 1 without window

top

SIDE
cut 1 with windows
cut 1 without windows

TOP
cut 1

MODERNIST VILLA PAGE 126

Templates are 25 percent of actual size—enlarge by 400 percent for full-size template (*see page 7 for copying instructions*).

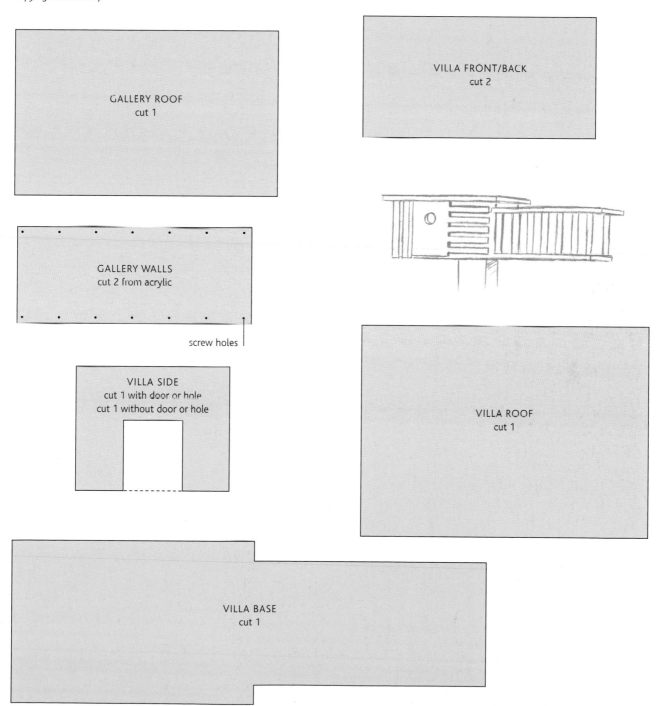

GALLERY ROOF
cut 1

VILLA FRONT/BACK
cut 2

GALLERY WALLS
cut 2 from acrylic

screw holes

VILLA SIDE
cut 1 with door or hole
cut 1 without door or hole

VILLA ROOF
cut 1

VILLA BASE
cut 1

Templates: projects

DINER PAGE 132

Templates are 25 percent of actual size—enlarge by 400 percent for full-size template (*see page 7 for copying instructions*).

DINER SIDE
cut 1 with hole
cut 1 without hole

DINER TOP
cut 1

HOT DOG BUN
cut 2

BASE FLAP
cut 1

HOT DOG
cut 1

DINER FRONT/BACK
cut 2

SIGN
cut 1

BANDSTAND FEEDER PAGE 140

Templates are 25 percent of actual size—enlarge by 400 percent for full-size template (*see page 7 for copying instructions*).

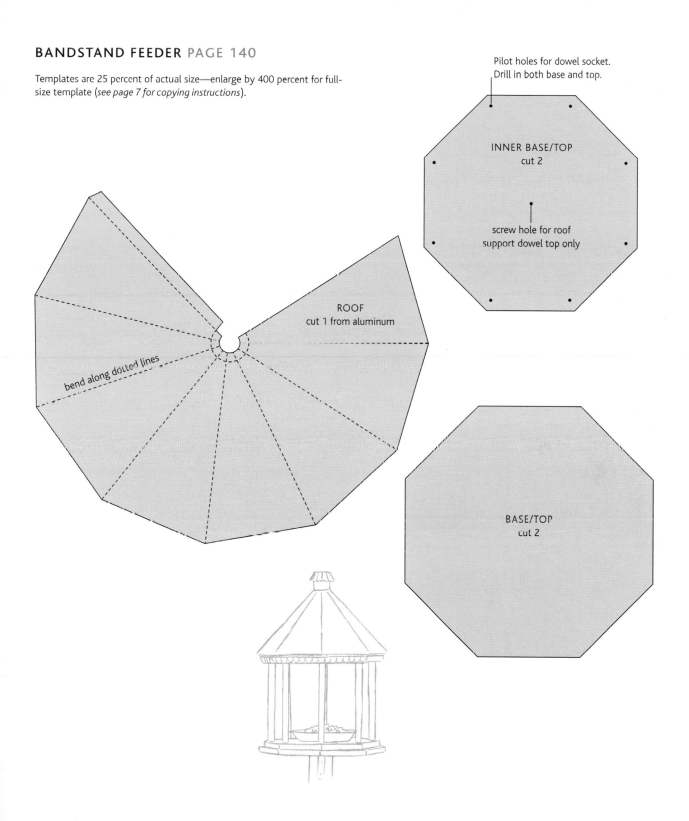

Pilot holes for dowel socket.
Drill in both base and top.

INNER BASE/TOP
cut 2

screw hole for roof
support dowel top only

ROOF
cut 1 from aluminum

bend along dotted lines

BASE/TOP
cut 2

Templates: projects

PADDLE STEAMER PAGE 148

Templates are 25 percent of actual size—enlarge by 400 percent
for full-size template (*see page 7 for copying instructions*).

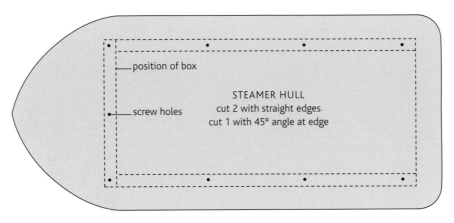

— position of box

— screw holes

STEAMER HULL
cut 2 with straight edges
cut 1 with 45° angle at edge

STEAMER SIDE
cut 2

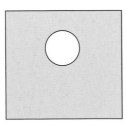

STEAMER FRONT/
END FLAPS
cut 1 with hole
cut 1 without hole

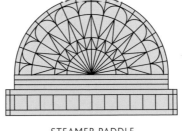

STEAMER PADDLE
cut 2

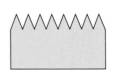

FUNNEL TOPS
cut 2

FLAG
cut 1

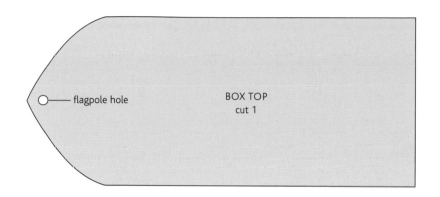

flagpole hole

BOX TOP
cut 1

UPPER DECK FRONT
cut 1 from ¼-in. (6-mm)-thick plywood

UPPER DECK
cut 2 from ¼-in. (6-mm)-thick plywood

LOWER DECK ARCH
cut 1

LOWER DECK FRONT
cut 1

TOP DECK ROOF
cut 1

TOP DECK
FRONT/BACK ARCH
cut 2

TOP DECK SIDE ARCH
cut 2

Resources

In the United States

NATIONAL AUDUBON SOCIETY
700 Broadway
New York, NY 10003
(212) 979-3000
Fax: (212) 979-3188
Web site: www.audubon.org

THE WILDLIFE CONSERVATION SOCIETY
2300 Southern Boulevard
Bronx, New York 10460
718-220-5100
Web site: www.wcs.org

In Canada

BIRD STUDIES CANADA
P.O. Box 160
Port Rowan, ON N0E 1M0
1-888-448-BIRD
Email: generalinfo@bsc-eoc.org
Web site: www.bsc-eoc.org

CANADIAN WILDLIFE FEDERATION
350 Michael Cowpland Drive
Kanata, ON K2M 2W1
1-800-563-WILD
(613) 599-9594 (Ottawa Area)
Email: info@cwf-fcf.org
Web site: www.cwf-fcf.org

NATURE CANADA
85 Albert St., Suite 900
Ottawa, ON, K1P 6A4
1-800-267-4088 or (613) 562-3447
Email: info@naturecanada.ca
Web site: www.nature.canada.ca

**NORTH AMERICAN WATERFOWL
MANAGEMENT PLAN**
Implementation Office
Wildlife Conservation Branch
Canadian Wildlife Service

Environment Canada
Place Vincent Massey, 3rd floor
351 St. Joseph Boulevard
Hull, QC   K1A 0H3
(819) 953-8458
Email: nabci@ec.gc.ca
Web site: www.nawmp.ca

Web sites
www.abirdsworld.com
www.americanbirdcenter.com
www.americanbirding.org
www.backyardbird.com
www.bestnest.com
www.bird-baths-buyers-guide.com
www.birdbooksdirect.com
www.birdfeeding.org
www.birdhouse.com
www.birdinfo.com
www.birdlife.org
www.birdwatchersdigest.com/
www.birdwatching.com
www.ibacanada.com
www.ornithology.com
www.worldbirder.com
www.wwf.org

For Further Reading

Books:
Backyard Bird Watching for Kids: How to Attract, Feed, and Provide Homes for Birds
George H. Harrison and Kit Harrison

*Bird Tracks and Signs:
A Guide to North American Species*
Mark Elbroch, Eleanor Marks, and
C. Diane Boretos

Birds in Your Backyard
Robert J. Dolezal

Book of North American Birds
Roger Tory Peterson

*Know Your Bird Sounds, Volume 1:
Yard, Garden, and City Birds*
Lang Elliot

*Manual of Ornithology: Avian
Structure and Function*
Noble S. Proctor and Patrick Lynch

North American Wildlife: Birds
The editors of Reader's Digest

The Sibley Guide to Birds
David Allen Sibley

Magazines:
Backyard Living
Birds & Blooms
To order these magazines,
call toll-free 1-800-344-6913

Index

Acknowledgments

Special thanks to Adrian, Daisy, and William.

The publisher would like to thank Homecrafts Direct (www.homecraftsdirect.co.uk) for the loan of props.

photo credits

The publishers would like to thank the following for permission to use the images listed below:

Front cover, page 28 (Eastern bluebird): © Joe McDonald/CORBIS.

Page 2: © James L. Amos/CORBIS.